PRAI

"What Nanci 'gets' is not for her; it is for anyone who comes near her. This book is an expression of generosity to the millions of us who don't know why we just don't like our mother. This book was written for that little boy or girl inside of all of us who missed something. Nanci wants you to have it back, and she wrote love onto every page for you to know HIS love in a fresh encounter."

—Rachel Faulkner Brown, Director and Founder, Never Alone Widows, Co-author of: *Father's House: The Path That Leads Home*

"In *Angry Daughter,* you will be supernaturally empowered to successfully navigate the painful emotional gauntlet of anger, shame, forgiveness, abuse, and fear. In vivid detail, Nanci recalls her painful past, then reveals a Holy Spirit infused strategy to take back what the enemy stole from her. In exploring her steps, I am certain you'll discover your own personal miracle."

—Tony Nolan, Pastor, Oak Leaf Church, Canton, GA

"...a detailed but incredible testimony of the lies the enemy attempted to plant in her young, vulnerable mind as a child. This story also reveals how Nanci was able to forgive, understand, and overcome. She turned an upbringing that could have crippled others into a passion to encourage and free others. What a story of God's amazing grace and kindness!"

--Marc Lawson, Pastor and Founder, VALOR Center, Holly Springs, GA, Author of *The 166 Lifestyle*

"Reading Nanci's story has helped me realize some of the things that I still need freedom and healing from myself. Nanci shares in such an honest and gentle manner. She helps create a safe space where considering my own past doesn't feel daunting. I am able to relate, and I can start to see which of my own memories still need to be given to Jesus."

—Jordin Early, Behavioral Therapist, Consultant, Speaker

"I encourage you to read *Angry Daughter* with a prayerful heart for what the Holy Spirit may show you in your own forgiveness journey. I do ask that it not simply be read but read and responded to. I encourage ministry leaders to explore using *Angry Daughter* as a book study for women's groups - teens, adults, and mixed age. Reader, the mighty grace of God is at work through this writing; welcome that work of God into your life as you read and respond. May it be so!"

—Rev. April Briant, Elder, Global Methodist Church and host of the *Unshakable* podcast

"*Angry Daughter* will bring healing and wholeness to everyone who reads! It is a journey through Nanci's life but really, it will be a journey in your own heart, your own past, and your own relationships. Your journey from hatred to love will begin the second you open this book! Her story reads like the grittiest southern fiction but pierces like the deepest surgeon's scalpel. Your healing will begin as Nanci unravels her story—which will change yours!"

—Amanda White, Author of *Truth in the Tinsel*

"A treasure trove of revelation to set your heart free."

—Karen McAdams, co-author, *Father's House Bible Study* and co-host of *There Is More*

ANGRY DAUGHTER

A Journey From Hatred to Love

NANCI LAMBORN

Angry Daughter: A Journey from Hatred to Love

Published by Bloomfire Press

Copyright © 2024 by Nanci Lamborn. All rights reserved.

No part of this book may be reproduced in any form or by any mechanical means, including information storage and retrieval systems without permission in writing from the publisher/author, except by a reviewer who may quote passages in a review.

All images, logos, quotes, and trademarks included in this book are subject to use according to trademark and copyright laws of the United States of America.

Scripture quotations marked (ESV) are from The Holy Bible, English Standard Version (ESV), copyright © 2001 by Crossway, a publishing ministry of Good News Publishers. Used by permission. All rights reserved.

ISBN: 979-8-218-37296-5

Christian Living / Personal Growth

Cover design by Wolf Design and Marketing, copyright owned by Nanci Lamborn.

All rights reserved by Nanci Lamborn and Bloomfire Press. Printed in the United States of America.

DISCLAIMER

I have tried to recreate events, locales and conversations from my memories of them. In order to maintain their anonymity in some instances I have changed the names of individuals and places. I may have changed some identifying characteristics and details such as physical properties, occupations and places of residence.

CONTENTS

1. Beautiful Sunset — 1
2. The Death of Shame — 5
3. Angry No More — 13
4. Details, Details — 21
5. The Smell of Fear — 27
6. Unsupervised — 33
7. Ceiling Beans — 41
8. Strays — 45
9. The Lie Bump — 49
10. Never Enough — 55
11. Thousands of Stitches — 61
12. Norman Rockwell — 67
13. Three Million Miles — 73
14. Missing the Music — 79
15. Death Basement — 85
16. Eyes to See — 91
17. We Be Fine — 99
18. Pain — 103
19. Vices — 109
20. Choosing — 113
21. Proud — 117
22. Portraits — 121
23. Love/Hate — 125
24. Forgiveness — 129
25. Iniquity — 135
26. Clean — 141
27. Heights — 145
28. Grace — 151
29. Not My Circus — 157

30. Real	165
31. Holy Anguish	171
32. Discovering Destiny	175
33. Grief	181
34. Sandra's Daughter	185
The Empty Chair Exercise	191
Author's Note	199
Resources	200
Additional Recommended Reading	201
End Notes	202
About the Author	203

This book is dedicated to my amazing husband, without whom my journey would never have started; to my twin sister who journeyed with me at every step; to Luci, who saw this book before it existed; and to my Lord Jesus Christ, who continues to do the impossible.

Chapter One
BEAUTIFUL SUNSET

Our handwriting was almost identical. I could forge my mother's name perfectly as early as middle school, which I did often. It came in very handy when skipping school to cross state lines with my boyfriend, which I also did often.

Our widow's peak hairlines were also similar. She could walk into my band camp rehearsal with her hair tied up in a high ponytail, and half of my classmates who had never lain eyes on my mother would look at me and say, "Your mom's here."

How often I hated her hairline, and the squinting angry eyes and tightly pursed lips that came along with it. Usually the ponytail meant she was on some warpath, and I'd better look productive or else. When she was trying to impress others, her dark, shoulder-length mop of baby-fine hair was curled and teased high, then well set with several passes of Agua Net Extra Super spray. When she was addressing the thorn in her side, which she often deemed her daughters to be, she needed her hair to be out of the way. It felt like she wanted to be feared, and she was.

She didn't seem to care much for my hairline either. There was absolutely no place for any sort of tenderness when it came to ". . . getting that nasty mess out of your face." Massive tangle or not, my mother wielded a hairbrush with the delicacy of a construction backhoe. She seemed to both despise the task of fixing my drowned rat hair and also love the fact that it hurt me. Her criticism was most likely her way of toughening me up for the hard realities of life, but I just felt like an unloved nuisance.

I hated her hairline back then. But not too long ago, I found myself stroking it in loving comfort, kissing her forehead gently as I whispered, "Well done, good and faithful servant. Go and enter into your rest with the Lord." And I meant it.

Her death at seventy-six was torture for her and torture for me to watch. Like many others who had trusted their doctors to recommend what was best for their health, my mother's body had reacted to this one particular injection with a swift and irreversible devastation. We and the ICU doctors could do nothing but watch throughout the day as Mom slowly bled out from the ruptured clots in her bloodstream. By the time the evening finally rolled around, any more efforts to save her life were clearly over.

Ignoring the bodily smells and undignified drool under

the ventilator tube taped to her mouth, I gently held her hand. I wasn't angry. In this moment I felt oddly proud to be with her, sensing the sacred honor of being present for her final hours.

"Remember this moment. Pay attention," the Lord said loudly in my spirit. Dad was home resting after his long day shift at Mom's bedside. My brother, Edgar, was too compromised to visit a hospital, and my twin sister, Jillian, lived out of state. So I was alone with Mom in her hospital room as a nurse changed out her IV. The nurse rounded the bed and glanced out the westward-facing window and said, "Wow! Did you see what the sunset looks like out there?"

I moved out of the nurse's way and sat down in the window seat. She was so right. The sinking sun was just at the tree line, a dark orange ball without a single cloud to compete with it. As I marveled at the shift from orange to blue to the first visible stars all in one frame, I heard the Lord again clearly as he said, "This sunset is beautiful."

The journey of the seven years leading up to this moment played across the movie screen of my mind in a flash. I realized that going from despising to loving to losing my mother could have been a vastly different story. I very nearly became one of the many tragic statistics who refused to deal with the wounds of the past. I had every opportunity to end up saddled with resentment and regret after burying my mom with lots of unfinished business to haunt me for decades. But the Lord in his goodness orchestrated otherwise.

I marveled at the beautiful sunset for a few moments, then turned back to look at Mom, her eyes closed and her breathing labored. My eyes brimming with grateful tears, I knew the Lord wasn't talking about the sky.

Jesus, I choose to forgive my mom for leaving us too soon. I forgive her for the grief and the pain and the hole this has left in our lives, and I forgive her for leaving Dad in such grief. I choose to forgive those connected to the chemicals that ended her life prematurely and left us with anger and injustice. I release all of this to you, Jesus, and I ask you to take all of this, and to come and heal my heart like only you can. In your holy name, amen.

Chapter Two
THE DEATH OF SHAME

*H*ow do we come to cherish a place where trauma and shame were born? Only by divine influence and radical healing.

As one out of every four little girls has likely experienced in America today, my childhood innocence was taken from me by a person who was close to my family. Shame is just one consequence. It is ironic that the definition of shame is a sense of humiliation or embarrassment that comes from the perception of having committed a wrong. We as victims of abuse are not guilty of any wrongdoing. We do not choose abuse, but as children we are wired to believe we are the ones who have done wrong. Our enemy convinces us as the child, the victim, that shame is ours to wear. I wore it as well.

Parenting by shame had been a common tool in Mom's upbringing. The cultural assumption was apparently that making a child feel more horrible about themselves would bring about improved behavior. I can only imagine my mother's heartbreak and embarrassment when, in front of the entire seventh grade, she was loudly singled out for a minuscule infraction by her mother, who also happened to be her American History teacher. Clearly that doesn't work for most children. It just makes us hate ourselves more.

My maternal grandmother was certainly skilled at using shame to control and condemn. As a child I only had to see Mom and Grandmother interact one-on-one a few times to recognize the underlying tension. It was clear that my mother was never able to earn the love and approval of her mother.

Because of her own insecurities, I believe Mom was ashamed of her children often. When we would fidget or giggle or talk in church, because of the status of her family within the church, she saw our actions as bringing great shame upon her. This fear of embarrassment also manifested at every family gathering. If we behaved as children typically do, acting like kids instead of mature adults, in Mom's mind, this brought shame upon her. Never mind the fact that we were still in elementary school. She expected behavior that our child-sized brains couldn't produce, and her response to this behavior would be to insult and correct us publicly, in front of her entire family. I suppose this was her way of deflecting the shame she believed was upon her so we would have to carry it.

It is ironic that because of the abuse I was enduring on a regular basis, I was already wearing shame like a favorite sweater. I now understand that in the brokenness of her own weight of shame, Mom could never see it on others, including those of us who lived in her home.

For roughly a decade, my dad's great-uncle Jack lived with my paternal grandparents three bumpy hours away on a piece of land they called The Farm. Technically it belonged to my dad's mother and adoptive stepfather, but the details of this fork in the family tree are filed amongst the Things We Never Discuss. Depression-era families were rarely known for their emotional vulnerability.

I'm not sure what they were supposed to have been farming. It's possible that this grandmother, whom we called Nonna, had named it The Farm because they still had to chop firewood for heat. I never once saw a single stalk of corn nor blade of wheat nor evidence of livestock. I did see endless winding gravel roads, sloping hills of rock dotted with dry, feathery grass, and creeks full of crayfish. The countless hours spent crossing those creeks and exploring the endless fields were full of rich wonder and fresh country air. Suburban kids could get gloriously lost for hours playing in that part of the world. I loved it.

The old house itself, the only home for half a mile in any direction, wasn't much to brag about. The single-story white country ranch had a wide porch that ran the length of the front and a rusting tin roof that sounded lovely when it rained. The wide wooden-planked floors always creaked, and the small living room featured a massive rock masonry fireplace along an entire wall. Over the decades, the home's foundation had settled unevenly, so anything round would always roll to one corner. Even the smoke from the fire smelled old.

Nonna was present but not present. She didn't have time in that house to dote on any grandchildren. My only memories of her at The Farm were of her anxiously serving the men in the room. She constantly tidied, cleaned, and refilled coffee and tea with the demeanor of a beaten slave girl in a king's household, ever fearful of some future wrath were she to miss a crumb. I never saw my grandfather or my great-uncle act in violence toward her, but the underlying threat was noticeable.

It was there at three years old that I also experienced my first exposure to abuse and a loss of innocence. My darkened memory includes my mother walking in on my great-uncle Jack, my twin sister, and me in his bed. There was some snatching up and a few cuss words, and in that moment it seemed my mother's heart turned against me. Mom was clearly enraged, apparently at me and Jillian since she said nothing; not to Uncle Jack, not to Grandaddy, Nonna, or Dad—she told no one. We knew we were in deep trouble, but we didn't understand why. After that happened, it never made sense to my toddler-sized mind why my mom's facial expression would turn to disgust whenever I tried to climb into my Uncle Jack's lap.

My parents were only affectionate on occasion when it

suited them, which wasn't often enough to suit me. As most children do, I enjoyed the love language of hugs and kisses. So despite the things done in secret, from which I learned to dissociate, I craved and sought after physical affection. But this made me "bad." Oh, how I hated feeling guilty over wanting a hug.

"Quit hanging all over Jacky!" Mom would snarl, as if I might transmit some kind of plague to him from my contact. I didn't have a description for this increasingly guilt-ridden sense that came from my longing to share affection. In my heart it was more than knowing I had committed a transgression. I *was* the transgression.

Both Grandaddy and Uncle Jack fell sick several years later, so they all moved back into civilization so Nonna could take better care of them. Grandaddy died before my seventh birthday. Uncle Jack shocked everyone by recovering, and then he decided to move into a house one block over from ours so he could "help my favorite nephew Herbert with things around the house." He haunted my world in secret for another three years.

I'm not sure if Nonna ever knew about what had been done to me and Jillian, but strangely enough, her world became lighter and brighter with widowhood. She hung floral wallpaper and planted huge flower beds, and she turned the interior of her house into a Sears & Roebuck catalog page complete with fringed chenille bed covers and ceramic Hummel figurines. And much to my surprise, Nonna began to truly enjoy the company of her grandchildren. But she rarely enjoyed the company of my mother, and this disfavor was openly mutual.

It would be almost forty years before I laid eyes on The Farm again. Other than seeing a black-and-white picture of the front of the farmhouse every few years when relocating a photo album, the place and all that happened there rarely crossed my mind.

Well into my deep spiritual journey, through which I was learning how to allow Jesus to heal traumatic memories, my husband Brian and I had taken a camping trip a few hours away from home. With miles of trails, rivers, and antique shops to explore, we took our time enjoying the quaint country scenery. As we rounded a particular two-lane bend, my heart started to pound.

"Oh my goodness! I remember this curve! The road to my grandparents' farm is just around the next rise. I wonder if it's still there. Let's go see!"

As my implicit procedural memory kicked in, I slipped back in time and precisely navigated the narrow, no-longer-gravel streets until my truck sat directly in front of that old tin-roofed homestead. Its wooden front porch, as ever, still needed a paint job. All of the beautiful rock and scrub grass which had once covered the terrain had yielded to the modern hand of development, as an entire neighborhood of small, single-family homes now filled the landscape.

It is only a testimony of profound divine grace that I could sit and stare at that house and appreciate it. In the many months prior to this unplanned visit, I had been intentionally pressing into the truth about myself as defined in the word of God, and I was healing. I had a keen awareness that the history of what had happened in that house could have resulted in my feeling anger, shame, and bitterness in this moment. But all I could feel was good.

The sight of The Farm brought waves of gratitude. Wonder. Nostalgia. Joy. While I did still have the distant memory of what had been done in secret, it simply didn't have any power over me. What was foremost in my mind was the recollection of hours of fun and country freedom. Everything felt right as the July sun sank over the trees behind me. It was all I could do not to take off running barefoot into the creek. But no need to traumatize the current occupants.

I realize today that Mom never seemed fond of discussions about The Farm. Sadly, she never thought to look for someone who could help her take her emotional trash to Jesus and allow him to dispose of it. So her emotional trash was forever mixed up inside. Even if there was a memory of joy and fun and sunshine, the odor of decaying garbage always wafted its way in.

Trauma that was never addressed is an especially stinky type of emotional baggage. It makes us jumpy and turns us hypertensive. If it isn't producing desperate avoidance, it oozes out as a toxic need to control absolutely everything. Mom was all of these.

I rejoice in the Lord for the disposal of my trash through the time with my soft and discerning mentor and the paradigm-shifting presence of Jesus. I can reminisce with laughter and thankfulness and a deep love of creek-crossed country land and tin-roofed farmhouses. Because trauma and shame had packed their bags and moved out.

Lord Jesus, I choose to forgive and release my Uncle Jack for violating me and stealing my innocence. I forgive both of my parents for not protecting me. I forgive my mom for failing to seek justice, for blaming me, and for turning in disgust against me. I forgive them all for the effects these had on my life. Lord, I ask you to heal the wound in my soul, and to cleanse me from all of the shame and trauma, and Lord I receive your healing. Amen.

Chapter Three
ANGRY NO MORE

It has been said that anger is most often the result of unmet expectations. Of all of Mom's moods I remember, anger was the most consistent in our home. My mom was very, very angry.

It never occurred to me to wonder why the Scriptures and sermons we heard every Sunday didn't translate into a Christ-centered, grace-filled home growing up. Now that I have been freed up from the religious legalism of churchianity, I understand that my parents were more concerned with ritual than Godly relationship. The lenses of spiritual abuse and the embedded hellfire-brimstone perspectives of the Lord turned the faith of my parents and their parents into slavery. It was all about rules of performance and appearing perfect in front of other believers. But this lack of intimate relationship with the

Grace Giver means that unbridled anger is perfectly acceptable if angry is just who you are.

One of my earliest memories of Mom's anger was of her stomping on me and Jillian. We accidentally woke her up on an early Saturday morning while watching cartoons on the living room floor. As siblings often do, we had become rowdy. With her puffy, baggy eyes, her Aqua Net bedhead hair, and her gritted teeth, she looked like a monster. I thought something evil had taken over my mom, and I was terrified and blindsided. We had been giggling like normal four-year-olds, but she took our infraction as an intentional offense done to purposefully rob her of precious sleep. Her level of rage as she towered over my small frame and smashed my legs into the floor made no sense, and once again I was transgression itself. Ever absent, Dad wasn't around to protect us (not that he would have done anything about it).

Being the pianist in our large church congregation, Mom was often angry at our behavior in church because her children were a direct reflection of her. Our church had been her family's only church for three generations, and close family members held positions of influence. Our tribe of five was always on display, so we already felt judgment around every corner. Countless stink-eye glares from the piano bench were cast our way during services, and we knew that a pinch in the hangedy-down part under the arm would be next if we didn't straighten up. We were pinched a *lot* at church.

She would often get angry even when we were supposed to be enjoying ourselves on a family vacation. We were too broke to afford many extravagant trips, so we would pile up all of the camping gear and haul our massive canvas tent to the state park campground for two weeks every summer. Our only source for an evening meal was whatever fish Mom caught from the lake during the day. Fishing while we camped was her only break from her kids, so she would be gone from sunup until sundown to chain-smoke and bring home supper. Dad would spend all of his time quietly reading newspapers or collecting downed tree limbs for the fire. But heaven help the kid who wanted to go find out where Mom was.

She was angry often, but nothing beats the rage in the letter incident.

The night before our high school graduation, Jillian and I felt on top of the world. We had spent very little time at home our senior year thanks to boyfriends and a two-hundred-dollar station wagon we called The Bomber. Edgar had gone off to live with Nonna while attending college, and we were chasing freedom with all we had.

Unfortunately, Jillian had begun journaling the year before as a way to process her emotions. She discovered the cathartic release that came with writing it all down so things didn't stay bottled up. She would write herself letters describing the feelings that she could never express, and then she would throw the letters away. Her writing included statements such as, "I hate my mother! She can't even fold my socks right! She stretches them all out and it makes my socks look stupid. I hate my mother's cooking! Her food is terrible, and I hate that she is so mean and fat!"

Daughters who journal their true feelings about their mothers should know never to throw away their work at home.

Jillian and I had decided to enjoy a nice dinner out with our boyfriends the night before our high school graduation ceremony. We were about ready for dessert when a flushed and wide-eyed waiter made his way to our table.

"Excuse me, is one of you named Jillian? There is an urgent phone call for you in the lobby."

Apparently Mom had decided to put something away in Jillian's room, and seeing a crumpled piece of paper in the trash can, she couldn't resist reading it. I wasn't able to hear the conversation on the lobby phone, but I could see the shock and rage on Jillian's face. She returned to our table and announced that we had to leave because she was being kicked out of the house.

The argument back at home was hard to make out from my room until they both escalated. At that point it was likely even our neighbors across the street could hear the fight. I had never heard Jillian try to stand up to Mom before; she had been using her journaling to do that. As I listened to the argument from under my covers, my heart sank as I realized Mom really was rejecting her favoritely named daughter. It was quite clear that Jillian was no longer welcome to live there anymore, all because of a few words on a discarded piece of paper.

At one point, Mom wailed, "I put all my hopes and dreams in YOU!" The pain and anguish and disappointment were palpable. It also pricked my heart a little that Mom had apparently had no hopes or dreams for me.

Jillian retorted, "Well, who asked you to do that?!"

Mom's response was to walk away, which she did often.

The moment graduation was over the next day, my twin sister was gone, and I was left alone with Mom and Dad. It's no wonder I jumped into marriage just a few months later. I saw it as my only way out.

Anger, bitterness, resentment, offense, rage. Our family had it all, mostly through Mom. The Bible refers to these destructive family patterns as "iniquities," and we are promised in Exodus as part of the Ten Commandments that they pass on to the next generations. They certainly passed on to me.

I deeply regret the expressions of anger that I exhibited after starting my own family. I had learned to slam doors, to scream and yell, and to throw things when something didn't go my way. I was simply demonstrating what I had observed. I knew no different.

The 1954 poem by Dorothy Law Nolte titled "Children Learn What They Live," which was prominently displayed on the wall inside my nursery school, explains it perfectly. The message was that children will demonstrate what they see in their family of origin, whether positive or negative. I saw that poem every day for several years. Even at a very young age, it saddened me that I knew something wasn't right in my house.

It took the wisdom and patience of a gentle, Godly man to put an end to all that nonsense. After divorcing my first absent, alcoholic husband and remarrying when my children were in middle school, my brand-new husband Brian came home to a raging fight between me and my tween-age daughter. I was taking out my anger on the environment as she and I screamed at each other through her locked door. Brian had never seen this side of me, and he was not about to normalize it.

But instead of joining in or trying to referee, he looked at me with love and gently said, "This is not how our household is going to go. You and I are going to get down on our knees right now, and we're inviting the Holy Spirit to bring peace."

Despite my bewilderment, that's exactly what we did. Brian didn't realize it intentionally at the time, but he had stepped into his role as the spiritual head of our home. He had taken his God-ordained, loving authority without ever condemning me, and a calm like I had never known settled over the environment.

Anger left my home that day, and peace took its place. Almost twenty years later, it's still here.

Lord I choose to forgive my mom for her partnership with rage and offense. I forgive her for passing these on to me, and I forgive myself for picking them up. I repent for holding onto anger and bitterness and offense. I renounce my own partnership with these, and I break their power in my life in the name of Jesus. Amen.

Chapter Four
DETAILS, DETAILS

Backless bedroom slippers don't function well as shoes.

I'm not sure how someone can let a car with toddlers in it roll unmanned down a hill twice in one day, but Mom apparently figured out how.

Picture this: slightly inclined driveway. Harried, tired mother still in her pink fuzzy slip-on house shoes. Car that may or may not have had a recurring transmission slippage issue and a parking brake located on the floorboard. Three screaming kids in need of a cold Yoo-Hoo from Nonna's fridge. Thankfully the corner stop sign saved us.

Distraction was a normal state in our home. When you have sixty-two choir members expecting their music to be sorted and ready, and you have just enjoyed your last Pall Mall menthol, and the dog threw up on the bed again before the kids were fully dried off from the bath, distraction makes sense. When in this state of mind, minor details scurry into a black hole until they sneak back out at 3:00 a.m. Details like proper shoes and parking brakes.

Other minor details include keeping the lit Pall Malls away from the lunch preparation area, or the whereabouts of your seven-year-old while slogging with millions of strangers at Disneyland, or the fact that your identical twin girls each have their own names. Realizing that your parents don't know your name brings a whole new level of unworthiness.

Minor details include the awareness that it's picture day, and that the "Keep On Truckin'" rainbow t-shirt with the spaghetti stain isn't appropriate for school photos, or which child is allergic to ketchup, and which child vomits at the sight of onions no matter how cooked Dad says they are, or which daughter has never, ever had a boyfriend, and which one has had four boyfriends in six months. More than a few times, Mom brought Jillian to tears by assuming that she was the one preparing for a date.

Minor details include remembering which pink bear is the third child's favorite and which pink bear is the dog's preferred chew toy, or which Tupperware holds the potato salad for the PTA luncheon, and which contains the science fair mold experiment. Many times, the Tupperware contents turned into mold experiments, whether there was a science fair assignment or not.

We all experience some level of fuzziness in life's details as we age, but Mom took it to record-breaking levels. It truly was revisionist history, or as we liked to call it, Sandra's World. It's funny-not-funny how the newly revised details always put her into a more favorable light.

In Sandra's World, she picked up the habit of smoking as part of a college sorority rush week dare. The reality is that her rebellion started with a stolen pack behind the Golden Gallon as a young teen, and sororities were for other classes of people.

In Sandra's World, her IQ increased ten points every decade, and by the time her highly intelligent grandchildren were in college, Sandra proudly claimed an IQ in the 160s. In reality, her intellect was the same as the rest of us.

In Sandra's World, Dad was chasing skirts on a business trip without his wedding ring while Mom was eight months pregnant, so she flew herself against doctor's orders eight hundred miles to straighten him out. In reality, she was lonely and fat and missing her husband as he attended days of job training in a dreary, snowy metropolis.

In Sandra's World, she handmade dozens of stunning floral silk arrangements for her granddaughter's engagement party after saving them from all of the weddings of her own children decades earlier. In reality, the small bouquets were premade bargain bin finds.

Exaggerations were the most extreme whenever she was within earshot of her many siblings. How else could she possibly earn their approval and respect? Mom spun many a tale to her sisters about her gourmet meal prep from scratch, bent over a hot stove for hours. In reality, boxed macaroni and cheese, overbaked fish sticks, and red Jell-O was on the menu at least once a week.

It eventually got to the point where I would just nod and go along with her story. Like humoring a preschooler who inflates her level of "helping" her mommy bake cookies, it just became easier to humor the storyteller. If one of my aunts would question Mom's version of the facts, I would just smile and find a reason to become scarce.

The wonderful thing about living in Sandra's World is that everything old is truly new again. She actually believed that she had never had a new towel, or a new car, or a new stove, or new cookware. Tableside guacamole, homemade coconut cream pie, and real fresh cut flowers for her birthday simply didn't exist within her records of the past. So it was exciting and new every year when she did in fact enjoy such things.

Now that she is gone, I've come to the place where I no longer need my aunts and uncles to know what the truth really was. They believe the stories Mom crafted, so they have built an image of her in their minds of a wife, mother, and sister who was skilled and talented and wonderful in every way.

Gratefully I am free of the need for them to know the whole, ugly truth.

Jesus, I choose to forgive my mom for revising history to make herself look good. I forgive her for feeling like she wasn't good enough or acceptable enough the way she was. I repent for judging her for this behavior, and Lord, I ask you to release me from the effects of my judgment. Amen.

Chapter Five
THE SMELL OF FEAR

I lived well over four decades before I learned that fear can actually be defeated. As good Baptists, we were all taught the Scriptures about the multiple commands to "Fear not!" And there's the well-known verse of 2 Timothy 1:7 which declares, "For God has not given us the spirit of fear; but of power, and of love, and of a sound mind." But these verses were ancient anecdotes believed only in that one-hour block of time spent inside the church walls on Sunday mornings. Those didn't apply to children who lived in houses full of darkness.

Our tiny house smelled nasty. Not nasty like old socks or wet dogs. I'm talking as in an unserviced portable toilet on its third summer after the Burning Man desert music festival.

This was partly because both of the dim and

claustrophobic bathrooms in our house were haunted.

The demon in the hall bath was in the ceiling. The combination light/exhaust fan unit had a large leaf lodged in the fan motor for well over a year, and when turned on, the exhaust fan sounded like an angry Sasquatch with a chest cold. When you are five and need to tinkle at midnight, this isn't okay.

We believe the haunting of the other bath all started around 1974 with that oh-so-entertaining game called the Ouija Board. Almost every family in America possessed this thing, including many clueless and easily influenced Christian families. Perhaps the board possessed us. Anyone unfamiliar with this "harmless" childhood diversion should search online and stream just a few minutes from the original *The Exorcist* movie for a quick education. This popular and supposedly innocent game provided "hours of family fun" according to the box, with each of us asking the talking board progressively darker and creepier questions, each convinced that the other was secretly pushing the eerie little wooden triangle thingy around the board. Cue spooky music.

One night that same summer, my twin sister had an encounter. In this very real event that my parents later insisted was a dream, Jillian walked down the long central hallway from the living room to the back of the house and through our parents' bedroom into their master bath. The window was filmy with Aqua Net and Pall Mall residue, and the room was so small that I could touch all four walls at once from the wobbly harvest gold-colored toilet. In Jillian's encounter, a ghostly severed hand hovered above the back of the toilet. After floating there for a few minutes, the apparition shot toward her, emitting an evil laughter through its fingernails. Jillian shrieked and darted down the hall and all the way out of the house. Then apparently she woke up.

However, the unexplained creepy coincidence was that my brother Edgar had The. Exact. Same. Dream. On the Exact. Same. Night. Cue *really* spooky music.

There was certainly no parental love or compassion to assuage our horror. Mom's lack of capacity to nurture meant that we were told to "shut up and stop with the wild imagination! You're being ridiculous!" But our fears were very real, and we were left, uncomforted, to get over it on our own.

To add to the terror of the old homestead, I distinctly recall one stormy night that same summer during which Jillian, Edgar, and I were in the basement rocking out to Heart and Electric Light Orchestra with our disco ball and black light velvet posters. A heavy lightning storm roared through the area, knocking out the power to the entire neighborhood. We were then stranded in pitch darkness with nothing to do but out-scream one another and run into cinderblock walls. Something that smelled of cigarette smoke mixed with Prince Matchabelli Night Musk grabbed my shoulder in the darkness, but I was too quick and didn't feel like being eaten, so I jerked myself free.

Later when the lights were back on, still laughing hysterically, Mom said she had been in the basement trying to help me. Despite her assurance, to me it was a demon.

Fast-forward a week or two for the culmination of the smell of fear. The Haunted Hand nightmare and subsequent basement terror was still shockingly fresh in our minds. The Ouija Board triangle had been very active in recent days. The fan that emitted the guttural howl still had a leaf jammed in it. And at two o'clock in the morning, seven-year-old Edgar really needed to tinkle.

There was no way he was going to face the Exhaust Fan Sasquatch in the hall bath, much less contend with the Haunted Hand in our parents' bathroom. So he cleverly found a viable alternative and stood over the metal heat vent on his bedroom floor to relieve himself.

After all of the scrapes and cuts that we had received from our playing like wild animals around those metal heat vents, one might say that Edgar exacted his revenge.

It turned out that he was not the only one of us to be so bathroom-resourceful in this same manner. We were brilliant, inventive, and terrified, and all three of us were on the Haunted Hand's hit list. So the nightly urine of three frightened children saturated the heating ducts of our very small house for many months.

Then when brisk fall weather set in and the furnace kicked on, our tiny house smelled nasty.

In general, children are much less sensitive to the

smells of their environment than their adult counterparts, unless the children are passing gas on one another on purpose or sniffing out the source of funnel cake at the fair. So that first chilly November morning when the furnace kicked on, we kids went about our morning pre-dawn routine as usual. Mom pounded on the bedroom door and yelled, "Up time!" We were shocked out of sleep and groggily began searching for something to wear to school, and we stumbled to the kitchen for cold cereal. A normal morning.

I only half-noticed the pained, nauseated, mystified expressions on my parents' faces. I gave little thought to why they went from room to room peeking under furniture, looking into closets and behind shower curtains, returning numerous times to the cat's litter box to lean over and sniff it.

That time of year the heat only came on in the early mornings since the afternoons were still shirt-sleeve weather. This same hunt-and-sniff exercise was carried out for several mornings in a row by my baffled parents, until one particularly frosty morning when Edgar decided it was just too cold to leave the warmth of his bedroom. He already had picked up the habit of sitting on top of the heating duct to warm up and s-l-o-w-l-y dress himself every morning. He figured he might as well relieve himself at the same time and keep warm. And thus he was caught red-handed in the act of fouling up the vents.

Mystery solved! Oh Lord, the commotion. Much

yelling, much spanking, much crying, more yelling, then off to school.

I often wonder how one removes a baked-in urine smell from a home's entire heating ductwork. Come to think of it, we did sell the house in the summertime, and I'm willing to bet that the prospective buyers didn't think to run the furnace before signing any papers. So if you are reading this and think that you were the unfortunate family that bought the Pee House in Decatur, Alabama, in 1977, we apologize, and we gently remind you to check the furnace for odors next time before purchasing. And I believe someone from The Travel Channel called. They're sending a crew from "A Haunting" to set up cameras in your bathrooms.

Thankfully, my houses of darkness are all confined to the distant past, having been exorcised and swept clean by much forgiveness and the cleansing presence of the Holy Spirit. Turns out, those Scriptures really did apply to me after all.

Lord, I choose to forgive my parents for never noticing the darkness and the demons in our house. I forgive my mother for laughing at my fear and for failing to comfort me. Lord, I give you all of the trauma and the fear, and I thank you for freeing me from the demons of the past. In the name of Jesus, amen.

Chapter Six
UNSUPERVISED

To a child, healthy amounts of supervision can feel like control and a withholding of all that is fun. As those children get older, they can usually recognize the benefits of that parental supervision and see it as the love it really was.

For the most part, we weren't bad children; we were simply unsupervised. To the outside world, these can often look quite similar.

There were no adults around to tell us not to play on the train tracks that ran behind our neighborhood. You would think we'd have had enough common sense not to line things up along said track, like Matchbox cars and pennies and dead baby possums, just so we could watch them squish when the train flew by mere inches from our faces. We were so close that we could see the fearful and annoyed scowl on the train engineer's face as he violently gestured for us to move back. Never mind the sparks from the train's wheels as they blew by closely enough to feel them sizzle in our hair. We were more interested in seeing the fruits of our labor than we were concerned about dying.

There were no adults around to tell us that while Mom was inside the church practicing, we shouldn't sneak into the church cemetery and use the mysterious graveside rituals our classmates had taught us to conjure up spirits. We had already been given that blasted Ouija Board by this time, bought for us by our staunch but clueless Southern Baptist parents no less. So the concept of conjuring was already formed through the encouragement rendered from the demonic cardboard sorcerer.

"Honey, who are you talking to down there in the basement with no lights on?" Mom called down the darkened stairs.

I yelled back hoping she wouldn't disturb us. "It's my new friend I met playing outside at church yesterday. His name is Odin, and he teaches me all sorts of things."

She was already walking away as she answered, "That's so nice. You kids have fun now. Herbert, where's my lighter?"

In that era, it was normal for us to be sent outside alone from dawn to dusk on the days we didn't have school. So we ventured for miles into the neighboring tracts of wooded land where we bicycled ruts into the paths we made. There were no grownups in sight who could shield us from the castoff stack of very adult magazines with very nasty, yet intriguing, full-color photos in them. How were we supposed to know not to pass them around to all the neighborhood kids?

There were no adults present to suggest we not turn that abandoned house deep in the woods into our personal play fort. Never mind that the second floor had completely caved in, that cat-sized rats were in abundance, and that several black and yellow signs with big words like CONDEMNED and DANGEROUS were posted all over. We traversed every inch of that house like raccoons on mission at a garbage dump. We spent hours jumping on the brown vinyl couch in what was left of the living room, until we found the cans of paint and decided the couch needed to be a new color.

Later, Mom leaned out the door into the garage and shouted, "Herb, have you been painting?"

Dad didn't lift his head from under the hood of the car. "No, dear, why do you ask?"

"I keep finding splotches of black paint everywhere," she griped. "There's some on the floor, some on the walls by the bathroom. There's even one on the pantry door."

Good thing we had tossed the rest of our paint-stained evidence out behind the next-door neighbor's garage. I heard later that Mr. Mitchell assumed his son had ruined his work shirt and grounded the boy for a week. I'm sorry, Stuart!

Devoid of adult presence, there was no one to warn us

not to turn my second-story bedroom window into a jumping launchpad. The massive patch of English ivy beneath my window was pretty cushiony, and we added some pieces of discarded window screen and several pillows to make it even softer. Never mind that the side yard was sloped, that the windowsill was twenty feet up, and that poison ivy grew in the side yard as well. As six-year-olds we voluntarily ejected ourselves out of that window like prison escapees who had heard a train coming. And then we did it again. And again.

Mom glanced sideways at me as I sat on the couch watching *Gilligan's Island*. "Did someone hit you?" she asked.

"No." I shrugged, scratching.

"Did you fall?" she asked, brow furrowed.

I looked past her, refusing to take my eyes off the TV. "No."

She looked closer, puzzled. "Where did all those bruises on your legs come from?"

"I don't know." I shrugged again. "Do we have any calamine?"

One of the problems with the lack of supervision was the regular assumption that the three of us were collectively guilty of wrongdoing. Gate left open and the dog got loose? Everyone gets a spanking. Rake went missing? Group spanking. Outdoor trash bin knocked over? Spanking. Never mind that the electric company meter reader left the gate open, and Dad forgot about loaning the rake to Uncle Ron, and a stray dog got to the trash can. The law must be enforced! So injustice became all too familiar.

One of the most memorable unsupervised moments was the paper Christmas village incident. Jillian and I were eight years old, and Mom and Dad had uncharacteristically left the house to attend some sort of social holiday function. They weren't just in another room to be quickly summoned in the event of an emergency. In fact, we had no idea where they were, nor were we given any way to contact them in such an event, as cell phones wouldn't appear for decades.

In the 1970s, Woolworth stores sold a disposable Christmas village made of cardstock paper cutouts. The buyer was to punch out the pre-painted shapes, fold them together on the dotted lines, tape the seams shut, and voila! Instant festive structures. Add some torn-up cotton balls for fake snow, and it was a magical winter wonderland.

This is all fine until the adults once again fail to follow the instructions about keeping open flames away from the décor. Mom had placed several tall cylindrical Christmas candles amongst the village, but she never told us not to light them. So on this December night, Jillian decided that the display, which sat atop Mom's antique buffet sideboard, needed to look more festive. So she fetched the matches from the fireplace and set to lighting. Being eight years old, Jillian didn't realize how fast paper matches would burn. So when the flames licked her finger with searing pain, she dropped the lit match into the artificial snow.

Edgar was playing with his metal Erector set down the hall while I was laying in my bed reading Nancy Drew. I heard a commotion, faint at first.

" ... help ... "

" ... fire ... "

"Help! NANCI! FIRE!! *FIRE!!!!*"

Edgar and I rushed out to find a terrified Jillian staring at a blazing fire where Christmas once sat on the antique furniture. Who knew that a surface covered with cotton balls would be so flammable?

Ever the quick thinker, Edgar ran into the kitchen to find something to put out the blaze. A massive, speckled enamelware roaster pan sat, full of soapy dishwater, soaking in the sink after Mom's head start on cooking the Christmas turkey. She couldn't have all of us hooligans underfoot while she basted a roasting bird on Christmas morning. So she had cooked it a few days ahead of time, stored the foil-wrapped slices in the fridge, and left the soaking pan to wash the next day.

I'm not sure how Edgar's gangly nine-year-old arms were able to haul that huge pan up out of the sink, much less into the next room and over to the fire. But Jillian and I watched impressed as the sudsy, still greasy turkey water was dumped onto the flames. And the floor. And the La-Z-

Boy. And Dad's stack of *National Geographic* magazines. No more fire! We were all so proud of ourselves.

Mom did not share our pride. "Why does the living room smell like burned turkey? Why is it all wet over here? Where did Christmas go?! If someone doesn't tell me what happened, every single one of you is getting a spanking!"

So we all received a spanking and were sent to bed without supper. And we never had a paper Christmas village again.

I am thankful that even with the lack of supervision, I can look back on these little moments and laugh, despite what wasn't there.

Jesus, I forgive and release both of my parents that they didn't realize how much their supervision was lacking. I forgive them for the times we were left alone when we were too young. I forgive Mom for not noticing that we conjured up spirits in the graveyard, and I repent and forgive myself for doing that. Jesus, I ask you to close every door that I opened, and I thank you that our house didn't burn down. In your holy name, amen.

Chapter Seven
CEILING BEANS

Beans were on the ceiling. Pork 'n beans, to be precise. About one-eighth of a cup in total dried mass above the large rear window in the kitchen that overlooked the backyard two stories down.

Blobbed and cemented into the corner crevice, half on the ceiling and half on the wall by the kitchen table, the pork 'n bean paint had been left to run dry, growing hard and dark. It was odorless and permanent, as much a part of the room as the light fixture or the back door. No one ever talked about who put it there.

We ate canned pork 'n beans frequently. I believe we kept the American bean farmers in business from 1972 until 1985, because this protein source was cheap and oh, so versatile. As an adult I now know better than to use them in chili and spaghetti and hot-dog/bean/cheese/ketchup casserole and soup and

Thursday Mystery Goulash. Growing up we thought everybody ate like that, so we didn't know better. And I can clearly recall wrestling with my sister over who would eat the single, half-inch square token of pork fat that always floated on the top of each newly opened can. That was good eatin'!

Chances are high that my big brother Edgar was responsible for the bean incident. Most likely he was demonstrating his ultra-intelligent nine-year-old perspective by explaining the plausible trajectory of semi-viscous brown liquids when launched from a levered metal alloy tablespoon atop the solid horizontal plane of the vermiculite table. This was how my brother typically communicated.

I can still picture the three of us eating there, alone, but not literally alone, since Mom and Dad were in the next room eating on brown metal TV trays to "get away from you kids." So we were merely supervisorially alone.

As with many other latchkey kids in the 1970s, we were left alone often. Many summers, even as young as age seven, we would wake up well after our parents had gone to work, find our own breakfast, pack our own lunch of Wonder Bread and Skippy peanut butter, then walk two miles alone to the community swimming pool. We would swim the entire day until the pool closed at 5 p.m. Then we would walk the two miles back home, arriving just in time for Mom to pull up into the driveway from work. She would stomp through the carport door and start cooking dinner, and we would hang up our wet swimsuits on the clothesline outside. Some days it was an absolute miracle that we didn't end up dead in a ditch or carted off in an unmarked van.

Around this age, we invented a dinnertime game we called Show. This activity was a frequent source of entertainment during which one sibling would cram their mouth as full as possible with the soggiest, most colorful morsels available, then summon another to peer at them from under the table and then "show" them the spitty contents and try not to laugh. We found ways to play this game at almost every meal.

Alone at dinner one particular evening, in the midst of a game of Show, Edgar whispered our favorite dinnertime words.

"Hey, girls. Watch this."

Jillian and I looked up from our under-table show, paused mid-chew.

As usual, Edgar wore no shirt. He checked mischievously for the grownups. All clear! His well-aimed balled fist was poised over the bean-laden spoon which he had balanced delicately on the edge of another upside-down spoon. His high-pitched voice whisper-yelled, "Bean!" as his fist came into contact with the utensil trebuchet.

PING! The wet blob of a mess stuck fast to the corner ceiling. Much laughter followed. Mom and Dad yelled from the next room, "Hush and eat!" But we heard no footsteps of impending doom, at least that time. Relaxing our shoulders in relief, we continued quietly giggling as we watched the saucy paste begin to coagulate in the warm kitchen, and we wondered if it would stay put. We giggled more in relief that it wasn't dripping onto Mom's favorite African Violet plant in the windowsill. That would have brought certain death.

Since Mom wasn't in the habit of paying attention to our facial expressions, she failed to notice the guilty aversion of our eyes and the biting of our lips to prevent laughter when she brought their dinner plates to the kitchen sink. A more observant parent would have sensed the cover-up immediately. Mom was a lot of things, but she definitely wasn't observant.

We wondered briefly how long it would be before a parent noticed the dried amber blob of protein on the colonial white ceiling and marched us all into the kitchen demanding the guilty party's head on a platter.

Like many of the other stains in our family, apparently never.

Lord, I thank you for the times you spared me from discipline after mischief. I forgive Edgar for the times he incited trouble, and I forgive my parents for the stains (physical and emotional) that were never addressed. I thank you, Lord, for releasing me. Amen.

Chapter Eight
STRAYS

Thump! Thump. Thump. Thump.

Three baby squirrels and their bushy-tailed mama landed hard on the hood of our car in rapid succession. We had just arrived home from church and were climbing out of the station wagon when the squirrel drop began.

Dad saw the issue immediately. A large black rat snake was slithering around a wide nest in the tree above us. It had apparently knocked its lunch onto our car. Sadly, the mama squirrel didn't survive the fall.

Mom's trauma-averse heart exploded.

"Oh, honey! Do something! They're just babies!"

Thus would begin yet another season of fostering a broken little creature. Turtles, bunnies, cats, dogs, and baby birds all found safe sanctuary at our house. Mom would say that critters sent to her house had come to heaven. For how much they spoiled their animals, fattening them up at their very own places at the table with fresh cream and canned tuna every day, that was about right.

The baby squirrels enjoyed extra special pampering. Dad decided to convert our orange 1970s freestanding metal conical fireplace into a cage. Never mind the mites and fleas and ringworm-inducing parasites. Let's snuggle and hand-feed these babies so that they become fully dependent upon humans.

Only one of the baby squirrels lived through the first night, and we named her Shirley. I'm not certain how anyone knew that she was a she. But Shirley lived in the fireplace for years until Dad decided she needed to live freely outside. She had never learned to forage for her own food thanks to our saving her, so my parents spent a few more years dutifully cracking open acorns and hickory nuts and other appropriate fodder so Shirley could live outside. She never did stray more than a few yards.

The problem with taking in strays is that no matter how much you love and pamper them, they are unpredictable and can turn on you. Poor Jillian is a walking testimony to this truth. Forty-two facial stitches and the near loss of her eye from a yellow tabby cat that Dad rescued from a bridge in the rain was proof that our parents lacked discernment.

When the strays are humans, the lack of discernment makes things significantly worse.

In the aftermath of Hurricane Katrina, well over 100,000 people left the New Orleans region and never returned. Many southern cities were flooded with Louisiana migrants who had lost everything, and one of these folks ended up on the front steps of my parents' Alabama church. After a four-minute conversation, my parents had a new house guest.

This house guest named Watinga was a six-foot-eight-inch-tall former resident of New Orleans's Lower Ninth Ward who had apparently just hitchhiked all the way from The Big Easy. Mom took one look at him and just knew that she needed to be his savior.

Within a week they had Watinga weeding gardens, repairing shingles, and polishing the church gymnasium. They also took him to purchase a new wardrobe, on credit cards that were already near their credit limit cap. They paraded this man around to friends and family like a newly adopted orphan baby. On one hand I was proud of my parents for being so helpful to a struggling, unfortunate man. It also stung a little that a stranger got a better version of my parents than I did.

After just a few weeks, Watinga and his new threads disappeared with my dad's pickup truck, wrecking it three states east. I think it took Mom months to admit that she had been swindled.

But Mom's heart for stray humans also had a different side. She would often be the only one to befriend the outcast, the lonely, and the homely people who drifted in and out of her church. Mom would give them labels like "Poor Widow Wanda" and "Hobbly Harriett" and "Big Man Bart" and "Old Maid Millie" when she would recount what she had done for them. It came across like a Boy Scout earning a merit badge for walking someone's grandma across a busy street.

But to her it was genuine. She would listen to their stories and weep with them in their pain and rage with them in their injustice. She would pray over them and hug their necks and call them family when no one else would. She would be Jesus with skin on.

And for a few moments, they would no longer feel like strays.

Lord, I thank you for the ability to reminisce without pain. I forgive my parents for every time they lacked wisdom and discernment. I forgive Watinga for deceiving them and for stealing from them after their hospitality. I repent for my judgment and lack of love for the people who Mom would show kindness to, and Lord, I receive your forgiveness. Amen.

Chapter Nine
THE LIE BUMP

Forget "sugar and spice and everything nice." We roamed the neighborhood with ice-pops and slingshots and handfuls of rocks. With highly active imaginations, we also concocted lots of wild stories and adventures. But sometimes the dirt and the made-up stuff became indistinguishable. And this brings me to the lie bump incident of 1972.

Part of growing up in the Deep South surrounded by many dozens of towering Loblolly pine trees was living with ticks. Each of our many dogs had one or two of the fat, shiny parasites lodged onto their ears or neck at any given time, and Dad would just pinch the nasty little thing with his massive fingers and yank. I'm sure his words included something about calling Mom as we enjoyed being grossed out when he dropped the flailing mass onto the patio and smushed it. It gave a satisfying crunch and offered plenty of kid-pleasing goo.

But amidst all of the bug-stomping fun, it never occurred to us there was even the remotest possibility of being afflicted by our *own* ticks. Until that dreadful day.

I was about six years old that spring, and as all good redneck children did in warm weather in Alabama, we frequently played outside in the backyard shirtless. Boys, girls, didn't really matter; shirts were not really a requirement if not in school or church or over at Aunt Betty's trailer (the really nice double-wide with the magenta shag carpeting and the brass and glass chandelier).

Anyway, our backyard was home to multiple massively tall and thin pine trees, where ticks had parties up in their boughs. The sneaky little critters would wait far up in the tree for their unsuspecting target, then let go to quietly sail downward. The poor shirtless soul below never felt the hit.

Landing stealthily on their victim's head or other exposed body part, the tick would immediately latch on to said prey and suck all their blood out and turn them into a three-eyed swamp monster from the *Food of the Gods* movie. Well, all but the swamp monster part. Only then would some furrow-browed adults somewhere mandate a rather painful tick extrication, to be performed without anesthesia, which required Mom's good tweezers, a just-doused match, and that horrible child-torture concoction known as mercurochrome.

This is assuming there is a recognition that the tiny black dot stuck to the child's body is, indeed, a tick. We knew ticks to be engorged, grayish, bean-sized dog parasites (like the size of the pork 'n beans stuck on our ceiling), not freckle-sized marker punctuation dots. Enter confusion, misunderstanding, and a needy and dysfunctional kindergarten classmate who knew very little about a very lot. We'll call this walking misprinted encyclopedia beanpole of a girl Betina.

At school one late spring day, Betina happened to notice something new and not quite right on my chest, just barely above the first button on my blue gingham blouse. Betina looked at my new feature with a condescending, worried look, then promptly informed me that this black dot was, in fact, a Lie Bump. She sternly asked if by chance I had told a lie, any lie at all, the day before. Why yes, in fact, I had. Most likely I had lied when Betina asked, as she did at least weekly, "Are you still my friend? Do you like my knee socks?"

Convinced of my transgression, needy Betina nodded wisely, saying, "Yep, that's a Lie Bump for sure, and if you cut it off . . ." She looked around the room for eavesdroppers before leaning in way too closely. Her voice dropped two octaves as her glare bored holes into my kindergarten soul. "You'll die!" And pulling up her socks, she skipped off to recess.

No way on earth was I confessing. I would sooner swallow a full tick than admit to lying. Surely Mom and Dad would subsequently demand to know every other untruth I had ever thought or spoken. Then no doubt one of them would rip the Lie Bump right off, bringing with it a certain instant and painful death.

Thankfully as a rule we were usually too-much-in-the-way around the house, so hiding was easy for a time. Mr. Tick stayed put and stayed fed, growing nicely over the next several days. But oh, the conviction! Each and every morning when I first opened my eyes, what was there waiting to taunt and tease and wave the banner of "LYING SINNER!" in my dirty face?

The evil bump continued to grow, so I decided to pretend it wasn't there. Easy enough. Baths were optional in our house. No need to waste good water. But somehow, although the details are blocked for probably a good reason, my parents eventually discovered the secret and immediately moved to dispatch it.

One would think that two full-grown adults who are intent upon tick removal would far outmatch a small girl intent on exactly the opposite. One would be wrong. I grew two heads and three extra arms and legs in my attempt to avoid being pinned down, but I lost the battle.

After being wrestled to the living room floor with Mom dodging my kicks and punches, Dad successfully yanked the nasty freeloader out, bringing a few bits of bloody kid-flesh with its pincers. My screams were proof that I believed I was being murdered. Edgar and Jillian sat on the couch wide-eyed, waiting to watch my life essence drain out of the Lie Bump crater.

Whew, that was a close one! Turns out it wasn't a Lie Bump after all, or if it really was one (which I still believed it was), removing them turned out not to be as deadly as Betina warned.

Slowly releasing his hold on me, Dad stood me up and turned me back toward Mom. "Honey, do you think she needs to be taking a bath more often?" he suggested.

"She's fine," Mom replied in her typically bothered tone. "Where's the mercurochrome?"

And by the way, Betina, I still don't like your knee socks.

Lord, I thank you that I can laugh at these kinds of things from childhood. I forgive my parents for not bathing us more regularly, and for being too distracted to notice what I needed. I forgive Betina for convincing me to believe a lie, and I forgive myself. I release it all to you, Lord, and I receive your healing. Amen.

Chapter Ten

NEVER ENOUGH

The spirit of poverty is a terrible family member to host. She convinces Mom and Dad that having fried corned beef hash and canned white hominy for dinner again is a great idea. She whispers words of fear mixed with instant gratification and unworthiness to ensure that every vehicle ever bought is guaranteed to have some catastrophic failure far before the auto loan with the 23% interest rate was paid off.

The five dental cavities before I started third grade due to the lack of toothbrushing, and the bouts of scabies and ringworm, were part of the picture as well. The people at the county health department never knew what to think of us. They had to explain to my parents why children should wear shoes when playing in a yard with dogs.

Poverty also demands the gratification of a street

urchin when any little gift is bestowed, and woe to that urchin if her display of gratitude wasn't gushing enough.

Before my late forties I never realized that one of Mom's top love languages was gifts. Like everything else over the top, Mom poured the very fiber of her being into the gifts she gave. Countless hours she poured into knitting massive afghans (which never advanced beyond their mid-1970s patterned colors, no matter the decade in which she made them).

Ugh, orange and brown chevron zigzag doesn't go with anything in my h— "Oh, yes! I love it! I can't believe you made this by hand! I know exactly where it needs to go."

The love language of gifts also made it impossible for Mom to keep a secret or wait until Christmas day. Had she not been permitted to sit the three of us kids down two weeks before Christmas with, "Close your eyes and put out your hands!" she probably would have burst into bits.

But then poverty had to have her say.

Mom's tone became accusatory before we had committed any crime. "Now these were *extremely* expensive. I spent over [name an amount most others considered appropriate but she considered criminal] dollars, so I don't want to find this someplace where it'll get ruined."

Cue required gushing and adoration from the offspring.

She did usually pick good and useful gifts, and we truly did appreciate them. But then she would mope on

Christmas day because the level of gushing adoration had waned.

Spirit of poverty, meet Pity Party Patty.

I now assume that Patty had consumed a drink or two before speaking up.

"I just don't feel like you appreciate all I've done for you and all I've sacrificed. I haven't had a new bra in seven years so I could buy you these things. And you just act so *ungrateful!*"

Cue weeks of depressed Mom moping and regular accusatory glares from Dad. It felt like I was set up to fail repeatedly because my thank-yous were never quite thanky enough.

The parental grumbling about running out of milk again, the anger when shoes became outgrown, and heavy sighing when a purchase was required for a school assignment regularly sent the message that there was never enough. Never enough money, never enough sleep, never enough time.

I also felt like I was never enough. My words, my cleaning and serving, my good grades. My very self. It was never enough. This constant awareness of lack was the very essence of poverty.

Another thing about poverty is that the list of debts are endless, and my mom was acutely aware of who was indebted to her. It was surprising what would turn into debt in her records, which could even include moments that were supposed to be fun.

Mom whispered in the dark as I slipped quietly out of her secondhand-smoke-filled wagon, "I'll wait up here away from the streetlight while you do the job. Don't leave the cardboard rolls behind; that would be rude. And for heaven's sake, be quiet! If you get caught, I'm driving away without you."

There are cultural rites of passage that every parent deeply desires for their children to experience. For some it is the first sleepover slumber party, or perhaps the first hunting or fishing trip. In my mother's family, it was the opportunity to go "rolling." That is the term we used in the Deep South for the act of vandalism whereby you completely cover a friend's (or enemy's) yard and trees and shrubs with as much toilet paper as you can find. Ideally this happens at night without being caught. In many areas today I believe this activity is considered a criminal offense, but for us it was the epitome of great, harmless fun.

The anomaly that was my mother beamed with a mixture of pride, pleasure, and rebellion as eleven-year-old me enjoyed the first taste of this kind of adventure. It commenced a several-year-long toilet tissue war between me and my friends, to see who could pull off the greater result without being caught. There's nothing quite like the thrill of seeing a perfectly launched two-ply fluttering over a crepe myrtle tree and landing in the perfect spot with a squeezably soft thud. We loved it.

But as with most things, there was a price to be paid

for the camaraderie. The facilitation of the event and the experience of the fun created an entry into Mom's log of debts. She had orchestrated joy for me, so I owed her. The problem was, it was never clear what would be considered as full payment of the debt. Her debt bank operated with compound daily interest, only I had never seen the fine print of this contract.

Perhaps this is what leads some of us into emotional bankruptcy. At some point, when the stack of unpaid debt gets too high, we just stop paying the bills altogether. The Bank of Mom didn't operate in my currency.

If the running debt list that she kept for her immediate family was large and ever-growing, the debt list that she held against herself before the Lord was immeasurable. More than a few times she mentioned that she considered herself personally responsible for a few very specific scourge marks on the body of the Lord Jesus Christ. In her heart, she saw herself as delivering the blows from the cat o' nine tails with her own hand, and she could never come to peace with the concept of grace and mercy.

I believe if she were to have defined forgiveness in the way that she actually walked it out, she would simply choose to bury it and never bring it up again. I understand much more now. Since she was never able to forgive herself and receive the forgiveness that the Lord paid for, she certainly couldn't have known how to pass that same kind of forgiveness on to other people.

This offended and frustrated me in my youth. Having

had no example of healthy forgiveness, I found myself obviously doing the very same things Mom did. Only now can I see with pity and compassion that she could never truly understand the message of the gospel of grace. She was unable to know that every single one of her debts really had been paid in full. She never was able to come to the place where she believed she was enough, and that nothing she did or didn't do would ever impact the Lord's love and acceptance of her. The more I grew in love for her, the more I grieved this for her.

It gives me great joy to know that she understands it now.

> *Jesus, I choose to forgive both my mom and my dad for partnering with poverty and lack. I forgive them for not being wise stewards with their resources, and I forgive my mom for her spirit of unworthiness and for how that impacted our household. I choose to forgive Mom that she couldn't accept what I had to give. Lord, I give you my offense, my frustration, and the judgment of my mom, and I thank you for releasing me from its effects in my life. Amen.*

Chapter Eleven
THOUSANDS OF STITCHES

The top of a six-year-old's head, when placed in contact with the open pointy end of a metal electrical fuse box door at a decent rate of speed, will slice open like a ripe tomato.

How do I know this? Jillian's head was the tomato.

A set of rickety metal bleachers were crammed up against the rear wall of the gym in a local school (that must have been built by the lowest bidder). Who would have thought to actually measure the height of said bleachers to make certain that the patrons sitting on the nosebleed row weren't in any sort of physical danger from, say, sharp gray metal objects that stick out?

Clueless person pushing the bleachers up against a wall plus clueless person leaving the large metal fuse box door ajar plus a wide-open kid badly in need of glasses results in screaming and bleeding all over the gymnasium.

Apparently my sister was forever attempting to release her brain from the confines of her skull, as proven by the above and reinforced by the hammer incident a year or so later. Hammers were always abundant and freely lying around at our house. We considered them to be playthings, and Jillian decided one day to play catch with one. Just as most children would safely toss up a tennis ball or a bean bag, Jillian thought that a hammer would do the trick nicely.

Except that Jillian needed glasses, or had lost her glasses, or had badly scratched her glasses, or had smeared them with something thick and gooey. This prevented her from seeing where the hammer might possibly land. Like squarely on the top of her head. She woke up several long minutes later with the headache from Hades, and the pine trees were spinning around like a magical kaleidoscope.

"Did someone hit you?" Mom asked, hauling my sister up out of the leaves.

"No." Jillian shrugged.

"Did you fall?" she asked, brow furrowed.

Jillian picked some leaves out of her hair. "No."

Mom looked closer, puzzled. "How did you cut your head?"

"I don't know. The trees are pretty."

And off to the hospital they went. "Hello, doctor, remember us?"

Children who need (and hate) glasses do not possess a keen sense of depth or distance. But in this condition we were encouraged, actually required, to go outside and play. We would hit that backyard of doom like squirrels on speed.

I remember trying to entertain myself one boring summer afternoon by bouncing backward down the two-story green concrete stairs that traversed the back side of our house. Somehow the green paint stands out in memory. The concrete was gray originally, but someone had painted it a dark forest-green "to match the trees." And it was forever chipping.

This particular day, the parents were at the usual place: Wherever Parents Go When Children Play. So no stern warnings were hollered from any open windows above to "act like a lady and quit jumping backward down the stairs!"

I bounced down the outdoor concrete stairs, facing the wrong direction, one step at a time, hopping and singing, "Delta Dawn" or whatever other pop radio tune was going through my head at the time. Certain that I had reached the bottom of the stairs, I decided a double-half-pike twisty turn would be a graceful way to exit the stairway and land—Ta-daaah!—on the patio.

Oh, how I was mistaken. My lower jaw came sharply into contact with the rusted metal handrail (also painted dark green to match the trees). I basically sucker-punched myself in the face with the railing. I think all of my teeth remained intact, but I can't remember clearly.

"Did someone hit you?" asked Mom, picking green

paint flecks out of my hair.

"No." I shrugged.

"Did you fall?" she asked, brow furrowed.

I ran my tongue over the bleeding split that was starting to swell. "No."

She looked closer, puzzled. "How did you bust your mouth open?"

"I don't know. The trees are pretty."

The backyard of doom contained toys and other oversized structures intended for hours of safe childhood play. However, when the directions for installation and safe use of these items was routinely ignored, injuries and excitement were sure to ensue. Large, top-heavy structures like the fifteen-foot, shiny metal sliding board, for example.

Jillian decided one morning that the small metal crossbars connecting the slide to its ladder would suffice as a pair of parallel bars to practice her gymnastics dismount. She had to jump up a few times to reach them, and then she could swing left and right, left and right, to gain momentum, and Wheeeeeeeeeeeee! jump off to see how far away she could land.

Seven-year-olds know little about physics. When a top-heavy item is thrown off balance, one had better make certain to be some distance away when it succumbs to gravity. Jillian was no distance away. The full weight of the metal monstrosity won the very short tug-o-war and came crashing down directly onto Jillian's neck.

"Did someone hit you?" Mom asked, wiping Jillian's tears.

"No," Jillian sniffed, pulling leaves from her hair.

"Did you fall?"

"No."

"How did the sliding board fall onto your neck?"

"I don't know. The trees are pretty."

After yet another visit to the emergency room, she was given lots of popsicles, lots of aspirin, lots of *Gilligan's Island* watching time and a new pink teddy bear. Jillian recounted how the doctors had held long minutes of hush-hush meetings with suspicious glances toward our parents. They finally accepted Jillian's story, thankful that she had not been beaten with a baseball bat. So there was no need to call protective services as they had first assumed.

The slide was convicted of assault and sent off for scrap. And only by the grace of God, we all lived to tell the stories.

God, I thank you for sparing our lives so many times! I forgive myself for my foolish behavior, and I forgive my parents for the lack of medical care and the unsafe playing conditions. Lord, I ask you to exchange my traumas with your healing and your peace. In your holy name, amen.

Chapter Twelve
NORMAN ROCKWELL

There's something about strolling through an antique shop or a flea market that makes me grieve and smile and wonder all at once.

One glimpse of a set of very specific fine china dishes or a yellow plastic coffee percolator and I am instantly transported back to Christmas at my great-grandmother's little house. I can still smell the home-grown green beans cooking slowly with a little sweet ham, ready to be plated next to her "creamed" potatoes that almost required a spoon. It was a Norman Rockwell painting in my mind.

My Nonna's china, with its wispy gold and brown pinecone pattern, was present at every holiday occasion. I'm not sure how most of it survived us often-feral grandkids. But today my own daughter is now proudly caring for that same special set of dishes, which we have enjoyed many a holiday.

I don't ever recall seeing Mom's fine china come into the light of day. It lived in darkness in the never-opened drawers of a heavy, scalloped cabinet off in the corner. The drawers themselves were so rarely opened that we had to shimmy-walk the heavy wood a centimeter at a time on each side to pull them out. This only happened the three times that Mom and Dad moved to a new house.

It must be hard to enjoy celebrations as an adult when Norman Rockwell is your standard.

Somewhere in her youth, Mom began to hold unreasonably grand expectations about special events. Thanksgiving, Mother's Day, graduations, family reunions, all of it. Weeks before the approaching day, an image would start to form in her mind of the perfectly staged photo that would mark the event as flawlessly glorious and fulfilling. She would dream of the pending event and make many hopeful comments about how she looked so forward to the coming special day. No doubt this mental picture included three rosy-cheeked, closed-mouth children buttoned up in their Olan Mills best while anticipating their mother's every need, as the (aunts, uncles, coworkers, church dignitaries) in attendance ooh'd and aah'd at the exquisite tablescape and my mother's elegant, graceful hospitality.

I cannot imagine the deep disappointment when reality unfolded. One kid loses her glasses and trips up the stairs, so blood is trickling down onto her white ruffled sock. Another kid gets carsick on the way back from the neighbor's house, and he starts gagging again at the smell of green beans, barely making it into the bathroom. And yet another kid has dropped Mom's only dessert onto the carpet and is trying to scoop it back together, cat hair and all.

Norman Rockwell, meet Moody Disappointment Judy.

Somehow Mom never learned how to go with the flow and laugh at the realities of parenting life. Her seasonal anticipation of let-down began to be so prevalent that as she grew older, she would fall into a clinical depression around the first of October. It wouldn't lift until January. She even began refusing to decorate for any holidays. If she couldn't have her Rockwell painting in real life, she wanted no part of it. She ended up begrudgingly adding a "Charlie Brown Christmas Tree," the eighteen-inch intentionally scanty tabletop scrub of a tree with a single droopy bulb. She would place it in the center of the kitchen table and comment, "That's just about right."

Strangely enough, she loved helping others create their own Rockwell scenes. She would spend hours setting up perfect tablescapes for the Mother's Day tea or the music department Christmas luncheon, or any other special occasion, as long as it was for someone else. She amassed over twenty large storage tubs of florals, greenery, and centerpieces from the many functions she decorated.

It was from those tubs that she and I had our best Christmas ever. After miraculously recovering from the devastations of the Covid virus at seventy-six years old, she was healthier than she had been in years. It's amazing what sobriety can do.

She had another holiday event to make pretty, and she actually wanted my help! We spent an entire day together, sorting, creating, and designing. And freely laughing.

At home that afternoon, I told my husband Brian, "This was the single best day I have ever had with my mom."

She would step into eternity less than eight weeks later.

The second Thanksgiving without Mom is coming up, and we are already planning the feast to be served on my mother's fine china at its new home with Jillian where it will be loved well and used often.

We will fully expect at least one dropped dish, at least one threat of barfing, and at least one bloody appendage.

But it wouldn't be our Norman Rockwell without it.

Lord, I choose to forgive Mom for her unrealistic expectations and for partnering with disappointment. I forgive her for never enjoying her own china and for refusing to decorate because she was pouty. And I forgive her that we won't have any more holidays together. I release all of this to you, Jesus, and I thank you for the healing that you are bringing to my soul. Amen.

Chapter Thirteen
THREE MILLION MILES

For most families, the concept of a smashingly fabulous time of fun did not include a cross-country July car ride with three prepubescents, one dog, and no air conditioning. But for us, this very description of excitement was exactly what we pursued. More than once. Yay.

Every long trip began in the same way, with Dad getting the car ready to go. Oddly, I don't ever recall packing a bag or suitcase of any sort; however, several well-stuffed, old hard-shell suitcases that smelled like Grandmother's bathroom were tucked away without our knowing. Apparently Mom expected that we might pack poorly on our own. ("How was I supposed to know I'd actually need underwear and shoes? Ow! But I do have something to cry about! Ow!") So crammed into that magical space-saving, mileage-decreasing invention known as the cartop luggage carrier pod, our engorged baggage was locked up tight, and Dad would summon us all to go to the potty and line up at the door with our pillows.

Dad had the ingenious idea of strapping all three of our mini-sized folding aluminum lawn chairs up onto the back seat with the safety belts. This grand plan achieved a much better-than-average view of the monotonous highway, a den under our backsides for Baron von Frisky (our mutt dog), and a built-in no-one-touches-anyone-and-I-mean-it barrier with the armrests of each lawn chair. No matter that the safety belts were securing our lawn chairs and not our bodies; that's what the pillows were for as far as we could guess, to cushion our carcasses in case they were ejected upon impact and sent careening end over end along with the vomiting luggage pod, down into a deep and bottomless gorge in West Virginia.

After bustling us up into the lawn chair wagon, Dad would crank each of the four windows down only about three inches and announce, "No touching!" We have no clue how that wee little air space was expected to adequately ventilate the hot air from our chatter, the secondhand smoke ash, and the egg salad gas emissions of us and the dog. So usually by the first picnic and potty stop, the windows were all down as far as they could go.

Our longest travel adventure by far was a July trek from Alabama to Montpelier, Vermont, to meet a newly revealed biological grandfather whose identity was never equated with a scandalous divorce, because "one doesn't ever talk of such things." All we knew was that he had a farm with a real hay barn and a horse, which all sounded quite satisfactory for us. But to get there, we had to endure a drive through seventy-four states and stop to take several photos in front of every landmark and tourist trap up the eastern seaboard.

These warm family memories captured in low-quality instant Polaroid film each depict a common theme. Invariably at least one child has been smacked, cuffed, or pinched in the tender part of the underarm and then forced to pose all familial in front of some monument or other. The convict is always easy to spot, leaning away, arms crossed, cheeks flushed, eyes moist, lips pinched into a you-better-smile-and-I-mean-it pose! We cannot locate one of these family photos where all five of us have a truly genuine smile at the same time. But the monuments all look rather nice, except for the photo of one rather noteworthy and historic monument of freedom that we presumably would have visited up close while on a northeastern seaboard jaunt. But, due to "too much traffic there," to us she appeared way off in the smoggy distance looking like an unloved Monopoly piece. From our lawn chair view, Lady Liberty was three-quarters of an inch tall and she smokes. "And lock your doors if we come to a red light around here."

The deeply southern family of five did finally bounce into Vermont, and the new grandpa with a horse and a haybarn was more delightful than we imagined. We did also learn many particularly important travel truths from this long trip:

1. Motel rooms in Rhode Island do not return any belongings left behind by guests, especially pillows belonging to children.
2. Baron von Frisky + apple + car ride = dog vomit.
3. July + egg salad + secondhand Pall Mall = kid vomit.
4. Dog vomit + kid vomit + map navigation = Mom vomit.
5. They don't sell any pillows north of the Mason-Dixon line. Mom said.
6. A week-long car ride as the only one without a pillow is very sad indeed.
7. If you can stay awake, watching the Big Dipper rise out the night sky window is pretty cool.
8. Meeting a new grandpa with a hay barn and years of pictures of us on his old pump organ is also pretty cool.
9. Egg salad gas emissions from kids and from Baron von Frisky smell exactly the same.
10. Montpelier is something like three million miles from Alabama.

Lord, I forgive my dad's birth parents for divorcing, and I forgive them and my parents for keeping it a secret for so long. I forgive Mom for carrying annoyance into our vacations and for the secondhand smoke. I thank you, Lord, for the sights we were able to see on this trip, and for the gift of recalling it fondly. In the name of Jesus, amen.

Chapter Fourteen
MISSING THE MUSIC

"That's supposed to be an F-sharp, Nanci!"

Mom could be frying pork chops in the kitchen across the house and know with complete accuracy which piano note sounded off-key. I didn't realize then how much of a musical savant she really was. Didn't everyone's mom routinely play Chopin and Liszt and Bach and Debussy on their own piano for fun? Can't all church pianists play any hymn ever written in church history, in any key, from memory, at a moment's notice?

The problem with knowing that F needs to be sharp is that there's no allowance for learning or failure. Great shame would result if I tried to pick out the latest Journey song on the piano, which unfortunately had exactly two chords and three melody notes and no more. Despite the annoying simplicity of the music, she couldn't encourage my trying. My mother's classically trained brain short-circuited at such poorly composed nonsense, and she couldn't bear one more note of "that garbage." So I would take a deep, offended breath, swallow my hurt again, and stop trying until she wasn't around.

Having a musically savant mother was not without its privileges. For any musical competition or variety show I was interested in, she was always available to be my accompanist with her massive library of fabulous show tunes. But she never believed that I could take first prize. She agreed to accompany me on the piano as the captain of the football team begrudgingly agrees to accompany the frumpy spelling bee winner to the prom. And the few times I did win, she marveled not at my talent, but at what might have influenced the judges' decision in choosing me as the winner. She never realized how much I needed her support and belief in my potential beyond being chosen as a stagehand. It was painful that my own mother couldn't believe in me.

Thankfully, the music did often include laughter. One particular Christmas I agreed to perform some traditional holiday songs at a large local holiday festival. While singing "'Twas the Night Before Christmas," I lost my place with the words at the precise moment when the lyrics refer to Santa Claus laughing. We both burst out laughing, and we couldn't stop. Then the audience laughed with us. She also had quite a jokester streak, especially on stage. She had a knack for complex pranks involving hidden scavenger hunt notes and complicit store clerks, and laughter was her fuel. She quite enjoyed leaving a peanut butter sandwich in a stage prop as I portrayed Miss Adelaide in *Guys and Dolls* at the local community theater.

As much as music was a constant companion of her soul, she never attempted to understand my music. She didn't seem to have the capacity to even try to appreciate my world of Amy Grant, Sandi Patty, Petra, and those early contemporary Christian songs that shaped so many of us in the 1980s. She missed out on the recognition that I was developing my own faith and growing in my own journey with the Lord. I was beginning to embrace his love for me and his relevance in my day-to-day life, but trying to share that with Mom felt like speaking a foreign language. As an extremely legalistic Southern Baptist, she had no spiritual grid for the Holy Spirit or a loving God who heard and moved on our behalf. In her learned cycle of religious performance whereby the favor of God was only achieved by pious slavery, she believed he might strike her dead if she didn't perform perfectly.

I believe that her ears were so attuned to the pitch, rhythm, and accuracy of the notes themselves that her heart completely missed the healing message. She couldn't fathom why I might have become choked up while singing the "Touch of the Master's Hand" about the dusty old violin that seemed worthless until played by a virtuoso. She did not have a grid for such emotion. She could recognize that it deeply impacted other people, but it always seemed to be a mystery to her as to why.

Time and infirmity eventually robbed those gifted hands of their capacity to produce exquisite music. Her beautiful baby grand piano remained, but except for a few cassette tapes and one CD recording of her, the music did not. Although she was incapable of expressing any level of grief over losing the physical ability to play, I'm certain that she continued to look for a place to escape within herself and numb the pain of this loss by regularly finding the bottom of a bottle.

At her funeral, which was attended by well over two hundred people, we took the time to enjoy some of the more extravagant pieces of music that she had once performed with ease. Then it was my turn to marvel at the responses of those in attendance who had never had the privilege of hearing these pieces played by my mother's hands.

Now that I have grandchildren, I find myself missing that music all the more. So I play recordings of it for them as I tell stories of the unique talent their great-grandmother was. On occasion while shopping these days, when a store's entertainment system cycles through to a very particular song by Franz Liszt, I pause, smile, and give myself permission to shed a few tears as I enjoy the music that I am now able to miss.

Mom, I choose to forgive you for not believing in me, and I forgive you for your legalism and for missing out on the Lord's work of grace and faith in me. Lord, I give you the hurt, the pain and grief, and I receive your comfort, love, and peace in return. Amen.

Chapter Fifteen
DEATH BASEMENT

Only two things in my childhood made me run really, really, *really* fast. The first was the happy, tinkling sound of the ice cream truck on a July afternoon. The second was being required to walk up the basement stairs alone.

If I didn't run up those open wooden slats of death fast enough, I just knew that the Haunted Hand would fly up after me and end my seven-year-old existence in some grotesque and gruesome slow method of torture. At any second I spent lingering on the stair, it would surely grab my terror-stricken little legs and pull me into Dad's pitch-black photography darkroom in the far corner, open its veins of battery acid upon me and engorge itself like a tick by consuming my flesh. Often I tried to run up the steps so quickly that I would trip over my own gangly feet and arrive at the top of the stairway bleeding from the shins.

My tears were more from fright than from pain, but I was relieved that I had survived the journey.

However creepy and frightening the basement seemed at night, it was equally entertaining and fun during daytime hours. It was a typical walk-out daylight basement, with a mismatched washer and dryer off in one lint-crusted corner, a makeshift darkroom in another, and a large billiard table in the middle. The pool table was in the way of everything and covered with a random scrap of foam. The hard concrete floor, which felt nice and cool to dirty bare feet in August, always seemed oddly damp as did just about anything else that had the misfortune of being kept down there. A huge chest-type freezer that always smelled of bait sat near the back door, and mounds and mounds of (also oddly damp) dirty laundry took up residence in front of the rusty-edged and off-balance washer. Piles of mildew-speckled boxes and books occupied the entire basement perimeter, placidly absorbing much of the worm-scented indoor dew that seeped from the concrete walls upon which paint would never stick. Spiders and millipedes loved this basement where they raised generations of their leggy families.

The stairs from this basement up to the kitchen were open on both sides, wooden and rickety, and the space underneath was framed out and used as storage for more pungent, speckled boxes. For some still unexplained reason, Dad was the proud owner of a box of what he called "Acid," which he stored underneath the basement stairs where everyone could access it, just as any safety-minded parent and homeowner should do. Dad wasn't a chemist to my knowledge, and he didn't strip furniture or floors for a living. So why he owned this death box remains a mystery to this day, other than he "might need it for something."

The symbols depicted on the side of this box were horrifying to my childish psyche. A simple icon of a large black liquid droplet falling onto a cartoon arm which was melting away from the droplet's impact was printed on the side of the box next to a red skull and crossbones. I didn't need to be able to read to know that this box would render all four of my limbs into stumps if I came into contact with its contents. So naturally I, along with my adventurous and brave siblings, made it our mission to throw random things into the fist-sized hole in the top of this acid box of death. But we were conscientious about our limbs, so we stayed at a safe distance as we tossed in broken crayon pieces, Barbie shoes, sucked-dry popsicle sticks, partial spools of thread, and the like. I refused to walk by that box under the stairs in case the acid became a living being and spewed some poison juice onto my bare feet and turned me into a paraplegic, so I always took the long way around it. Always.

The pool table was an intruding yet useful piece of furniture to have around. We never once used it for a real game of pool. If we even owned a single pool cue or some billiard balls, we never saw them. We did have a triangular ball rack, though, which came in quite handy for ringing the neck of a sibling and dragging her through the basement where she didn't want to go. But no, we used the pool table for much loftier undertakings. It served as a slumber party bed for us on many nights. We learned that if we slept up on the pool table in lieu of the floor, the roaches were less likely to crawl all over us. It was also the Bionic Woman operating table upon which my brother operated on my sister to make her bionic. I don't believe that the operation was successful, though; I'm sure we'd have been featured on the news or something.

After the straight pin incident, I was fairly certain that Mom also used the space as a sewing table on occasion. In this incident, Jillian was crawling across the pool table on her hands and knees, probably being bionic, when the next thing we knew, she was screaming and pointing to a shiny silver straight pin lodged inside her kneecap. Way, way in there. It was her own fault apparently, given the volumes of parental yelling involved during the less-than-sanitary pin extraction. Edgar and I hoped we might be able to watch her bone marrow leak out of the hole in her patella, but we were disappointed.

The basement darkroom Dad built for his short-lived photography hobby no doubt housed one of the world's Thirteen Entrances to Hell. Everything including the lone small window was painted pitch-black. The single bare hanging light bulb designed for film development was a ghastly dark red in color, and the chemical smell permeating the room was strange, sharp, and slightly nauseating. This den of darkness was where the Haunted Hand lived during the day, waiting to kill us all in our sleep. The Hand's younger cousin, Voltergeist, also lived there, hidden in its nest within a mysteriously open and unprotected light socket mounted high up near the ceiling. We could only access that fixture by climbing atop the photography worksurface, hopefully without knocking over the open jars of developing fluid. Voltergeist had a mystical hypnotic capacity that lured us in on more than several occasions, convincing our weak minds to dare one another to reach a finger into its uncovered hole and risk its jolting bite. We were never disappointed with the tingly result.

I never did outgrow my dread of that basement because we moved away from the monster-infested dump heap before we were old enough to figure things out. As far as we know, the Haunted Hand and Voltergeist are still there, scaring the snot out of the other children unfortunate enough to have moved in after us.

And one final note to the parents who either saw fit to purchase this particular home or who have some subterranean dwelling-level comparable to this. If you send your children to the basement during a tornado and the storm knocks the power out, be kind enough to take a flashlight with you to retrieve the little screamers from the pitch-black darkness. A single touch from a non-illuminated but well-meaning parent will result in children running blindly into concrete walls and knocking teeth out. Because Voltergeist and the Haunted Hand live there, and they don't carry flashlights.

Jesus, I thank you for cleaning up the darkness in the basements of my past. Thank you for the freedom to laugh. I forgive my parents that our basement was dark and scary, and I forgive my dad for his lack of safety precautions. Thank you, Lord, for healing my past. In the name of Jesus, amen.

Chapter Sixteen
EYES TO SEE

Hatred is a very strong word, but it fits. Hearing myself say that I hated the very air that my mother breathed sounds cringe-worthy, but it is absolutely true. For the many years in which I was focused on my trauma and offense, hatred became a constant companion. Back then I would not have labeled it as hatred; probably more annoyance or irritation dramatized with an eye roll and a deep sigh. Part of me believed (and still does believe) that my mother also hated me until later in my adulthood. She did her best to bathe, feed, and clothe her children, but she had to make sure we knew how much these things cost her. I now see that her definition of love and what a daily expression of love should look like was very broken and distorted.

One of our greatest needs as children is to be seen for who we are, to be known and heard and loved the way that

God made us. But nothing of the sort occurred in my mother's own upbringing. Now I understand that she was never taught to speak the language of being seen.

Six-year-old Edgar yelled at Mom from his seat at the kitchen table, "You don't love us!"

He and Mom had been having some sort of parent-child turmoil during dinner when Jillian and I were about five. I heard later that this accusation came because he had begged her to buy him a toy for which there was no money. I'm sure there was more to it. But my brother's statement reverberated with extreme truth, and my mother had no capacity to process what was said. It had nothing to do with a toy, and she knew it. So she took a long, sad breath, glared at her children, and left without saying a word. I think she even packed a small bag.

I remember seeing Dad's terribly angry, shocked face as he said, "There went the only thing I ever loved! You'd better hope she decides to come back!"

So much responsibility upon the shoulders of a child. And he only loved *her*? Message received loud and clear. Then, true to form, Mom was back in the kitchen making breakfast the next morning as if nothing had ever happened. No one ever spoke of that incident again.

I now recognize that it was very unsafe for her to see the real me. Truly seeing me would have meant acknowledging my trauma from the ongoing abuse. She would have noticed my lack of safety and my deep self-hatred and shame, for which she was partly responsible.

The risk of seeing me also brought the risk of my possibly being better than she was at a given task or that I may succeed in an area where she did not excel. That risk was too great for her.

But just as much as my mother was unable to see and know me, I was also unable to see and know her.

My incredibly gifted mentor Cyndi sat across from me, with the aim of leading me into Godly wisdom and understanding of my mom. Cyndi and I had developed a comfortable relationship after meeting in a small home group organized by our church, and I loved her immediately. After having pegged the source of my offense and obvious emotional baggage, she offered to take me on a prayer journey.

"Okay, Nanci. I want you to close your eyes and ask the Lord to give you a mental picture of your mother with new eyes. Ask him to show you how he sees her right now."

I had never considered such a thing. A trapped and wounded animal has no concern for the emotional state of its captor. It simply wants out with a vengeance and will fight desperately to do so. But the Lord is tender and gracious, and he gives us what we ask for in humility.

What the Lord showed me when I asked for this picture broke me, and I was forever changed. The image the Lord painted in my mind was dark and dreary, with a traumatized fifteen-year-old girl in the corner of her closet, shocked and grieving, with no comfort or tenderness after learning of her daddy's sudden death. She was shattered, bewildered, hurting, and utterly alone. As the Lord began to unpack the image for me, almost at once, every missing puzzle piece slammed together in divine understanding.

How do fifteen-year-olds behave? They're dramatic, petty, and moody. They complain, they're jealous, they need constant affirmation, and they must be the center of attention at all costs. Reconsidering every family gathering and every holiday and every milestone moment with this awareness of Mom's emotional age made everything make sense.

I could also see that fifteen-year-olds weren't prepared to be mothers. They are still children themselves, with unfulfilled dreams and desires to have amazing experiences in life and to know excitement, independence, and adventure. They are most certainly not ready to be responsible for three small children in a very small house with very small money.

I had never seen that the deep hole of grief in Mom after the tragic loss of her beloved father at fifteen had to be purposefully covered and buried at all costs to prevent the risk of leakage or exposure. With the new revelation, it began to make sense why she was never able to shed a single tear at a funeral, even the funerals of her own mother and brother and sister later in life. Because if a tear of grief might escape for them, an uncontainable flood would erupt, bringing a tsunami that would destroy everything.

I never had eyes to see that the voicelessness and powerlessness she experienced in her family of nine was partly to blame for her complete incapacity to take any action to help her own daughters when they were also voiceless and powerless under abuse. I didn't recognize that her fear of the risk of vulnerability brought with it an expectation she would then be in debt to someone else, and that was a risk she was not willing to take.

When I began to realize the life-altering truth that I actually was fully seen, purely known, and deeply loved by the Lord, I could then take the risk of looking at my mother with new eyes. And in the last few years of her life, I was able to see her for who she really was.

What I saw was beautiful.

Only a few short years later, I sat with my sister, Jillian, on the edge of Mom's bed in intensive care, trying to ignore the annoying beeps and weird smells. Mom had a look of wide-eyed wonder as she said, "The children with pink faces sing the most beautiful music. And the tall, shiny man said that I could go with him and hear it more closely if I want."

Jillian and I looked at each other. We knew this meant Mom wouldn't be with us much longer.

My mom's mother heard it first, the most glorious choral vocal music. She had heard it for a week or two before she stepped into eternity. And she saw the hand of her husband reaching through the ceiling a few times to invite her to join him, until finally she was ready to accept his invitation and leave this earth. Nonna had heard it too, in the weeks before she passed. She complained about the loud radio music blaring through the house and the people all singing and talking about the Lord, and, "Why can't they turn that down just a little bit? They're all just a little too excited."

Mom began to decline quickly once the children with pink faces started to visit and sing to her. As her bodily systems began failing and she lost most of her ability to speak, in the moments when her face would convey pain or discomfort, I would ask her if she could still hear the music. Immediately her expression would erupt into the most glorious smile, and she would relax into peacefulness as the music that only she could hear ministered to her.

I am so grateful to the Lord for giving me eyes to see my mom as he saw her, especially in those last hard days when her body was shutting down and stealing her dignity. I didn't have the same view that the nurses had; an obese, disabled, broken old woman. I saw her spirit, alive and regal and ready to finally meet her Lord.

And in his merciful goodness, he gave her eyes to see small glimpses of the glory that awaited her. We can only imagine what she is seeing now.

Lord, I repent for all the years I carried hatred toward my mom. I choose to forgive my mom' for becoming stuck and for making me feel like she hated me. I forgive her that she was incapable of seeing me. Lord, I release to you all the shame and unworthiness and anger that came as a result, and I ask you to pour your truth and your grace and your healing into the depths of my heart. Amen.

Chapter Seventeen
WE BE FINE

Mom learned her facial expressions from her mother, that rotund and legalistic matriarch of a grandmother whose duty in life was to judge and correct anyone in a thirty-foot radius with prideful disdain.

There was Mom's you-disgust-me-why-do-you-even-exist scowl. Then there was the I-wouldn't-be-caught-dead-anywhere-near-this-thing-you-chose shrug. And most prevalent of all was the we-be-fine face.

We've all seen this face. Lips and eyes plastered in a Sunday church directory smile while behind the scenes her fingernails were digging into whatever exposed, tender flesh she could find in the name of discipline. This fake face was the one appearing in every family reunion photo and at every church picnic. "Things are great! Pay no attention. We be fine."

Mom actually began to use this phrase out loud. They're going through bankruptcy again, and their church is going through a painful church split, and her favorite sister has just had emergency surgery. But we be fine.

She needed this statement to be true more than any other statement ever made in history. Because if things weren't fine, that meant we had to face them and (*gasp!*) perhaps even discuss them.

When your daddy, your person, the light of your life drops dead from a heart attack when you are fifteen years old the way Mom's father did, you have to tell yourself you're fine or you will not survive. I know now that Mom had no other option. Emotions in her home were as welcome as a cornered skunk. So she told herself she was fine until she mostly believed it.

But "we be fine" doesn't work when you learn that your own daughters are still being fondled by your husband's uncle down the street. At least, it shouldn't. But Mom made it work for her.

She could never understand why "we be fine" never worked for me. Seared into my memory is a question she asked twelve-year-old me after social services came to our house and blew off her "we be fine" lid.

"Was it really so bad that you had to tell somebody about it?"

Forty years later, I still don't have a good place to put that question, other than into the hands of Jesus (which I didn't learn how to do until a decade ago). But in that moment, like yeast in warm sugar water, my seething and indignation bloomed.

She didn't have a good place to put my answer either. "I told you about it a long time ago, Mom, but you told me to make it stop."

Cue the you-disgust-me scowl. And that was that.

Mom's "we be fine" continued in public places. Church. Her job. Extended family gatherings. But for a while it stopped working in private. She stopped eating. She would disappear for hours into the basement to play on our Pachinko vertical pinball machine and chain-smoke. She started seeing a secular therapist who only heard Mom's version of the truth, while no mention was made of arranging therapy for the children who had been violated and traumatized for years.

Then her drinking began.

I was confused and curious about the bottle of Southern Comfort I found stashed in the back of the linen closet. In our teetotaler Southern Baptist home, this didn't compute in my teenage brain. But if Mom was great at anything, it was hiding. And liquor made Mom feel fine indeed.

Mom spent the rest of her life escaping from reality in every conceivable way. Whether it was burying herself in a new wallpapering project, or taking on extra work hours to fold and stuff mass mailings at the kitchen table, or drinking an entire bottle of rum on the floor of her closet at midnight, escaping from reality became her survival tool.

It saddens me now to realize that her true source of escape was right beside her all along and she never looked for him. The manifest presence of Jesus as Immanuel God with us was always there for the taking, ever offering solace and healing and comfort amidst disappointment. But her fierce need for self-sufficiency and her fear of truth continuously lied to her and told her that she was just fine alone.

I love that the origin of the word *fine* has the Latin root word *finis*, which is defined as "end, utmost limit, highest point." It feels more appropriate than Mom realized.

I am forever grateful to the Lord that he continues to lead us toward a heart of wholeness in him despite our earthly circumstances. And I rejoice in the knowledge that today, Mom is indeed fine.

Jesus, I choose to forgive my mom for her need to keep up appearances, for her performance mindset, and for burying truth and walking in denial at my expense. I forgive her for every time she chose to hide in a bottle. I reject these for myself and my descendants, and Lord, I ask you to continue to make your tangible manifest presence known. Amen.

Chapter Eighteen
PAIN

"**D**on't you think these cramps could just all be in her head as a way to get attention?"

Mom winked and nodded at the doctor as she asked this question, leaning in as if trying to convince him to agree with her statement. I was there as a preteen to address an ongoing issue with extreme monthly cramping, excessive bleeding, and debilitating feminine pain. But because my mother had never experienced a period cramp in her life, there was no way she could believe that my pain was real. If something had not happened to her, then it couldn't possibly be happening to anyone else.

The season in which Mom and I made this visit to the doctors to address my horrible monthly cramping was just at the beginning of recognition in the OB/GYN community of what actually happens inside the ovary and the uterus during a release of an unfertilized egg. It turns out that the transaction is actually quite violent. Mom swore it was psychosomatic.

She never showed much compassion for injuries or woundings. I remember being chastised for using too many Band-Aids when I had to take care of my own long, deep scratch. She noticed them in the middle of a Wednesday night supper at church. She took such shame at my wound being publicly visible to her fellow congregants that she forcibly held my arm under the table.

Injuries were also costly. If I cost something, I was bringing inconvenience to the family. I am assuming that her own mother considered injuries to be costly in the same way, as my mother's first reaction when being severely burned by scalding water as a child was to run up to her bedroom and hide the rising blisters under her blanket.

When an injury was serious, Mom had an interesting phrase. She would say, "Well, you did a really good job this go 'round." And it wasn't a tender statement. I think she meant to be humorous, but underneath was an unspoken reminder: *You've really done a number on our finances this time. I hope you're proud of yourself.*

It also seemed that one should be ashamed when one has an accident. She had a devastating car wreck when she hit a patch of black ice, and she totaled her car plus two others. She was banged up but otherwise not terribly injured. She cried for several days telling the family repeatedly how sorry she was that she had done this. She apologized profusely any other time she had a serious illness or any kind of accident.

When she had another serious car accident where she ruptured two vertebrae in her spine, she began to understand the need to receive compassion for real pain. And despite having trouble ever believing that others really had pain, she grew frustrated and cynical when doctors wouldn't believe her or listen to her pain. Her injuries were severe, and the doctors who misread her X-ray films for months made things catastrophically worse. It's a sad irony that no one would listen to her.

Placing a stainless-steel spinal fusion cage into the body of a chain smoker is also catastrophic. While it kept her spine from further injury, it never resolved the pain. Like so many others who have walked this road, her existence became centered around the dozens of daily meds and a cane to support her crooked frame.

Eventually she needed others to physically experience her pain. More than a few times, when explaining yet again how bad it was, Mom would demonstrate by digging a finger violently into my hip joint with a stabbing thrust, intent upon inflicting the worst possible sensation to "show me what it feels like." Despite my being a believer in her pain, she needed me to hurt as she hurt.

But she didn't need this validation in front of important people. Her pastor, her neighbor, the cable technician, and the nail salon workers all saw a positive, determined, prayerful saint who laughed and loved hard and wept for orphans in Brazil. Perhaps in hindsight, she couldn't trust such outsiders with the privilege of causing them to feel pain along with her. I suppose this should have made me feel esteemed. In truth it just made me feel wronged.

It was interesting that throughout my childhood, Mom demonstrated a high tolerance for pain. But that changed drastically through her transition into full-blown infirmity. The slightest bump or scrape in the later years of her life would bring about quite dramatic wailing. She wanted to retell how the injury happened and receive validation. It felt similar to how a toddler responds to a skinned knee.

One of the hardest parts about the days leading up to her death was witnessing the amount of real physical pain she was in. It came to the point where only keeping her semi-comatose would ease the torment. It was excruciating for us to watch.

How often pain, whether emotional or physical, makes us feel helpless. We feel this whether it's our own or the pain of others. Mom's assumption with pain was that God had ordained it, and it was her cross to bear. It's sad to know just how wrong she was about that.

My Bible tells me that the Lord is close to the brokenhearted, and he heals them and binds up their wounds. He comforts us in our trouble, and I can call to him for help and he heals me.

I am so grateful that I knew where I needed to take my pain.

Lord, I choose to forgive my mom for the lack of nurturing and compassion. I forgive her for making me feel shame and guilt when I was hurt or sick, and I forgive her for every time she inflicted pain to make her point. I give up all of my rights to judge Mom's reasons or motives. Jesus, I release all of these things to you, and I ask you to cleanse and heal me from the effects these have had in my life. Amen.

Chapter Nineteen
VICES

"I had a bottle of coconut rum in the cedar chest, have you seen it?"

Mom asked me this with a groggy voice and heavy eyes, less than twenty-four hours after being released from a twelve-day hospital stay. She had been given dicey odds of ever leaving there alive.

Almost fifty years of smoking will do a number on the human body. She hadn't even tried to hide this habit in my childhood in the 1970s. Lots of people smoked. Then as the truth came out about tar and cancer in the lungs, she began hiding it. She never figured out that loading up on Prince Matchabelli Night Musk body spray after a smoke never fooled anyone. Dad even tried bribing her with a wood-paneled station wagon in exchange for her pledge to quit. That interior wood trim and the plaid cloth seating held onto that smoke smell like carpet holds onto glitter.

We were too smart to ever question why the wagon smelled like a dirty ashtray.

One of the worst parts of mom's inability to quit was the unmistakable aroma of Pall Mall released when I would open up my brown paper lunch sack in the middle school cafeteria. There's no flavor quite like a handful of second-hand-smoked Charles Chips.

"What is that smell?" A classmate across from me gagged. "Is someone burning trash?!"

For a season I actually smoked cigarettes as an adult myself. I had experimented with smoking through elementary and middle school, and, despite her own addiction, Mom knew enough to be sure to lecture me about adult-level decisions. Then when it was my decision to take up smoking in my twenties, Mom and I would sneak off together for a puff.

There's something uniquely bonding about having a smoke and a cocktail with your mom as an adult. This unspoken realization of grown-up-ness mixed with rebellion hits you both, and the relationship changes a little.

It wasn't until she had almost died from pneumonia after a COPD diagnosis that we all realized how bad her habits had become. As Dad spent his time at her intubated bedside, Jillian and I took to thoroughly cleaning their house, hopeful but not certain that she'd even live to see it.

Her smoking room, a small guest bath, revealed itself with

a single wipe of the interior linen closet door. Years of smoke and ash and Night Musk buildup disappeared in a stroke, leaving a bright white clean streak surrounded by dingy yellow. And just like my smoked potato chips, the towels in the linen closet were well infused with eau de Pall Mall.

We weren't sure what was worse: the inside of the secret smoking room or all of the liquor bottles. In drawers, behind shoes, under blankets, between cereal boxes. They were everywhere. And many of them were already empty. There's a pain that comes with this kind of discovery that is hard to explain.

Mom's doctor had issued an ultimatum. Absolutely no more smoking. Mercifully, she was in a coma during the physical withdrawal, so her body had done the hard part. The reality of having to be on oxygen for the rest of her life also turned out to be a pretty powerful deterrent for never smoking again.

It took almost dying from Covid and being forced into nursing rehab to actually get free of the drinking. She was angry that I'd had the nerve to tell all of her doctors that she was an alcoholic. She had told them she likes a little drinky-poo every once in a while. But her secret was out. Suddenly, her doctors had an answer for the many questions they had often asked about her recurring issues and unhealthy bloodwork.

After the third person in a white coat mentioned that she needed to quit drinking, Dad finally agreed to stop buying the stuff. Once she worked past the hardest part, she actually got sober.

To everyone's amazement, she became emotionally and physically healthier than she had been in many decades. She improved to a point where she needed less medication. She wasn't as angry or anxious or weepy. She became someone who was enjoyable to be around. I never thought I would experience this from her.

She would still joke about certain drinks that she really liked. But she would sheepishly admit that she knew she couldn't have it, and then she'd responsibly change the subject. We were so proud.

It may seem odd that the extended family gathered after her memorial service to raise an alcohol-filled toast in her honor, but the icky-sweet and fruity rum drink she would have loved made perfect sense.

Lord, I choose to forgive my mom for smoking while she packed my lunches. I forgive her for partnering with addiction, for hiding it, and for dishonoring her own body. In the name of Jesus, amen.

Chapter Twenty
CHOOSING

It's hard to keep choosing someone who rarely chooses you. It may be just as hard to choose yourself when you have heard all your life that your choices are wrong.

There's a delicate line in mother-daughter relationships where personal preferences and intrinsic value either fuse together or divide. Like the multitude of tracks in Grand Central Station, some of the lines merge together, never to separate again, while others split off completely. For some mothers, including mine, if my track wasn't her track, there was a hefty price to be paid.

"What do you want, leather?!"

Mom barked as I turned down yet another of her bra recommendations in the K-Mart dressing room. Never mind that her barely B cups had never had to fight against the entire eighth-grade football team the way my curvy C cups had. I had disagreed with her. So I was wrong.

Most of my life I had known that Mom wasn't chosen by her mother either. The demanding and rebellious middle of nine children, Mom was labeled the black sheep of the family before her tenth birthday. Grandmother even made a yarn art wall hanging of a mother sheep and her nine baby sheep in tow, and all were white except sheep number five. The yarn depicting that sheep was black. We thought this was funny as kids. It grieves me deeply today.

So, as many unchosen daughters do, I stopped choosing my mom in my early teens. Of course the emotional penalty payments continued until I escaped from the house for good only a few days after my eighteenth birthday. I was learning an immensely powerful tool of control, and I was choosing me.

I couldn't choose us both, and choosing me was empowering. But instead of the deep internal freedom I expected, a subtle bondage began to form. Label it resentment. Bitterness. Judgment. Anger. Unforgiveness. Or all of these rolled together. Choosing only me meant that I was also choosing those fruits of the enemy, only I didn't know it. The enemy is a crafty one.

As I continued my healing journey decades later, the Lord was so gracious to give me one last opportunity to choose her. After Covid had completely taken away Mom's ability to even grasp a pencil and had wrecked her body and her mind, the facility assigned for her rehab turned out to be ill-equipped and unsafe. Dad wasn't in the right headspace for caretaking, so I chose to bring a hospital bed into my home and nurse Mom back to life.

This choice to become a caretaker was made with a surprising level of grief and compassion. Never in my wildest dreams would I have seen myself voluntarily agreeing to take care of my mother. But in the season leading up to this, my heart had been shifting. I no longer needed to choose myself exclusively for the sake of self-protection. The Lord was rewriting my truth. It turns out I actually could choose us both in a healthy way. It felt like an honor to choose her.

Imagine bringing home a newborn, and she's addicted, obese, disabled, incontinent, annoyed, and heavily medicated. It was one of the hardest months of my life.

But amidst the constant restroom accidents, the alcohol detoxing, forced physical therapy, and barely touched pudding cups, I became aware of a supernatural shift that had taken place. I had chosen her, and I hadn't regretted it. I had chosen her in her hardest hard, and it turned out to be a truly beautiful gift for me.

Mom, I choose to forgive you for every time you didn't or couldn't choose me, and for the pain this caused. I forgive Grandmother for never choosing you and for labeling you as the black sheep. I forgive her for what that did to you. And I repent and forgive myself for holding onto anger and resentment. I release all of it to the cross. Amen.

Chapter Twenty-One
PROUD

"She had no idea who I was."

As I took off my chaplain's lanyard and recounted this hospital visit to Jillian, I marveled at the mystery of the human brain. As a chaplain I could enter into Covid lockdown wards when no one else could, and I needed to see Mom with my own eyes.

Blame the poor lighting, the medication, the Covid fog, or my rarely seen professional attire, but Mom welcomed me into her hospital room like she was welcoming Pat the Longhorn's Steakhouse manager who had stopped by to ask if the ribeye was tasty.

It was strange. I saw what the rest of the world usually saw, not what I knew. I saw a stiff upper lip, a self-deprecating deflection, and a slightly false humility that she should warrant such an honored guest as this hospital chaplain. As her daughter, I knew that fear and confusion and loneliness were the real truths. But she wasn't about to share that with Pat.

I marveled at something else even more. When I as the "visiting chaplain" asked her how I could pray for her, she started talking about her daughter in ministry. *Me*. And, shocking as it was, she talked about how proud she was of me. *My mother was proud of me.*

As a resentful and brash sixteen-year-old, there was a distinct moment where I chose to speak my true feelings about the absence of feeling parental pride. This was dangerous in our house, so it was rare. The lead-up is fuzzy, but the complaint was distinct.

"When was the last time you said you were proud of me?!"

The fallout is also fuzzy, probably because our brains tend to block the traumatic moment of impact to protect us. But experience proves that my declaration of truth was either met with indignant huffy silence, loud and teary dissertations of self-sacrifice, or reminders of how much I cost—or all three of these mashed together.

Had I been Edgar the golden boy, that question would never have formed inside my head. In our family, our culture, and most other demographics in my circle, boys were simply more valuable. A sister could have vacuumed and put dishes away and changed the cat litter without a blink, but a brother received a standing ovation for placing a towel near the laundry hamper. Combined with Mom's typical words of corrective criticism and snide remarks, it left very little room for me to feel that I was a source of pride.

This history added to the sense of wonder in me as a fifty-two-year-old hearing that my mom was actually proud of me. Even though it wasn't me she thought she was telling, she was telling it nonetheless.

I wasn't very proud of Mom throughout much of my life either. For many seasons I was actually embarrassed by her. Her flamboyance in a crowd, her lack of an oral filter, and her complete inability to pick up on subtle cues were all humiliating. And there was the one time that she actually forgot to wear pants to Easter dinner.

But in choosing to let the Lord teach me the freedom of releasing the past, I was shown more about her true heart. It was this truth that I shared with the world at her memorial service.

I could not have been more proud.

Lord, I choose to forgive my mom for not knowing how to be proud of me growing up. I forgive her for favoring my brother and for how much hurt this brought me. I break agreement with the lie that I am not someone to be proud of, and I break the power this lie has had on my life. Amen.

Chapter Twenty-Two
PORTRAITS

I have never met another person who wept at being presented with a framed photo like my mom did. And I'm not talking a single sweet tear in the corner of her eye. I'm talking a shoulder-heaving sob.

I now understand that one of Mom's love languages was gifts, and somewhere along the way she had connected the gifting of a portrait as equivalent to the gifting of one's actual self. So whenever she received a portrait as a gift, she was receiving the gift of that person's very existence.

When someone hates themselves as much as my mother did, allowing someone to take a picture of you is a sacrifice more costly than death.

Mom's self-hatred apparently set in early. She was the wild, unruly, clumsy child. She was the only one of her many sisters whose hair and lips weren't naturally perfect.

She was the heavier sister with the buck teeth and the embarrassing acne scars that no makeup could cover. She was the rebel whose disapproving mother still judged well into adulthood. She had many reasons to hate herself.

Most of the family photos from Mom's childhood looked forced and uncomfortable. All nine of the children were lined up chronologically with stern Grandmother at the head, and each face bore the required formal but joyless expression. From the stories I've heard, there was little reason for joy there.

This attitude about Mom's picture being taken is quite evident in most of our annual family photos growing up. Unless someone was able to snap a candid moment when she was really laughing, most of her expressions were a tight-lipped, manufactured smile.

My dad knew how much Mom hated posing for pictures. So it was particularly shocking one Christmas in my mid-teens when Dad unwrapped a professional full-length portrait of her. She had willingly fixed herself up fancy, taken herself to a portrait studio, and had framed this photo and given it to him.

I realize now that he comprehended what she was doing.

This gift had come just a few years after everything hit the fan in our house when social services came calling. She had chosen to blame my dad for what Uncle Jack had done. She held him responsible as if he himself had committed the abuses. She had needed to blame someone she could punish, and Uncle Jack had already died by this time. Dad was the easiest one to blame.

My dad had chosen to humble himself when everything came out. He moved away from religion, and he drew closer to the Lord in real faith. He had truly softened and grown spiritually.

He had also, much to my shock, apologized and repented to me and Jillian for the abuse we endured. He sobbed openly, acknowledging that he had failed to protect us, and asked for our forgiveness. His genuine brokenness and humility made it easy to forgive him for his absence. He became different.

Mom had most definitely not softened. For many months after the social services exposure, she refused to even touch my dad. She would drop dinner on the table without a word, go into another room, and close the door. I didn't see them exchange more than a few cold sentences for weeks on end. She withheld herself completely from him.

Through time with her therapist and humble patience from my dad, Mom's coldness began to thaw. Eventually she allowed reconciliation to ease its way in, and their relationship began to restabilize.

So in her own way, this gift of a full-sized self-portrait was communicating to him that she was giving herself, her whole self, back to him. The way my dad wept clearly showed that he understood the message.

Thankfully, her aversion to photos began to wear off as

she aged. In most of these pictures in later years, her hair is a disaster, her clothes are stained, she's forgotten to wear a bra, and she doesn't look beautiful by the world's standards. But she does look authentic, and sometimes even joyful.

The very last photo I have of her was taken in the hospital two days before she passed. Jillian and I took turns posing at her bedside, and after Mom and I smiled cheek to cheek at the camera, Jillian captured an unplanned moment. Mom turned her face up to me and puckered her lips for a sweet, grateful kiss. With her hair sticking out, her ugly hospital gown, her arms bruised from too many IVs, and her face all splotchy, I kissed my Mom.

I cherish her whole self every time I see that picture of us.

Mom, I forgive you for hating yourself so much. I forgive you for being averse to including yourself in photos. I forgive Grandmother for not loving herself and for teaching you the same. I give up my right to judge you, and I release you to the cross. In the name of Jesus, amen.

Chapter Twenty-Three
LOVE/HATE

"Why don't you just go and off yourself?"

I'm unsure how a mother could ever utter such a devastating phrase to her own flesh and blood, but mine did.

Mom and my brother, Edgar, abhorred each other but only within the confines of Mom's living room. In public they were best buddies. Mom had never severed the umbilical cord with Edgar, so the codependency started early. She also emasculated him with her smothering, and the clear favoritism at the same time ended up creating a monster—an entitled, frustrated, aimless, angry monster.

Edgar was also stuck emotionally at around the age of twelve. Although he didn't feel safe enough to reveal this to our parents until decades later, Edgar had been molested by a pedophile neighbor in junior high school. As is the case with millions of other tragic statistics, this season of trauma fundamentally changed who Edgar was. So Mom as the stuck fifteen-year-old and Edgar as the stuck twelve-year-old ran the household while constantly sparring to be king of the hill.

This kind of codependency doesn't work well when the adult son gets married.

It's a bit of a shock that Edgar ever married in the first place, but choosing a wife who was even more broken than he was made it easy. His wife Wendy was, for all intents and purposes, an orphan.

The poor girl definitely didn't sign up for the package deal that she ended up with in both Edgar and Mom. Wendy and Edgar immediately moved into Mom and Dad's house, where they all lived codependently until babies came along.

No one except Edgar was surprised at his eventual divorce. Entitled, angry, frustrated husbands who still live under the oppression of their demanding mothers can often become abusive themselves. And to Edgar, the end (total domination) justified the means (violence).

Of course Mom (who "never liked that Wendy anyway") was thrilled to have her son back under her roof, until she realized she had a twelve-year-old, and he realized he had a controlling and bossy mother. Like two ticks with no dog, they sucked the life out of each other. Dad tried to escape from the constant turmoil by working more hours. He couldn't reason with either one of them, and neither one would listen, so he just stopped trying.

After Mom relayed one particularly abusive verbal attack from Edgar, Jillian and I tried to step in and force Edgar to live elsewhere. Then Mom was riddled with guilt, and despite hours of counsel from everyone, she let him move back in to continue the chaos. My frustration with her was constant.

It was strange how Mom and Edgar would praise and defend one another to friends and family in public. But behind the front door, it was downright nasty.

Dad relayed the worst confrontation to me in a phone call. I'm grateful I wasn't present.

"You have never been a good mother to me!" Edgar had shouted. "I can't ever do anything right! I can't even take out the trash right! It's your fault Wendy left me! It's *your* fault I'm like this! I HATE YOU!"

Cue Mom's tears.

"After all I've done for you?" she sobbed. "Here we are trying to retire, and all I ask for is a little help around here, and you don't even notice the cobwebs everywhere. It's all my fault I guess. I'm just a terrible human being and an awful mother. If things are so bad, why don't you just go off yourself?!"

Cue slamming doors and days of silent treatment.

Edgar never did try to hurt himself. I guess most twelve-year-olds don't have it in them thankfully. But sadly enough, he developed a chronic kind of blood disease that began to slowly destroy his life. This particular condition, I learned later, has been scientifically connected to people who deeply hate themselves. Edgar clearly did.

How quickly the imminent threat of death can make us put our differences aside! But the forgiveness that Edgar needed to extend did not come until it was too late.

I remember holding him as he wept at the helplessness of his inability to visit Mom when she first contracted Covid. Because of the lockdown and his own compromised immune system, he was forbidden to enter the hospital. My heart hurt for him as I felt the weight of his regret and his worry.

I held him again when he couldn't come to her bedside in the final days of her life. Underneath all the rage and bitterness and codependency was a little boy who desperately needed his mom to know just how deeply he loved her.

She knows now, Edgar.

Lord, I choose to forgive Mom for her codependency with Edgar, and for how this harmed and dishonored our whole family. I choose to forgive Dad for his passivity and his absence. I forgive Edgar for holding onto bitterness and for the hateful fights they had. I release all three of them to the cross, and Lord, I ask you to cleanse and heal me. In your name I pray, amen.

Chapter Twenty-Four
FORGIVENESS

I had heard many times in church that Jesus commanded his followers to forgive. He delivered his parable of the wicked servant who was forgiven a large sum of money but then wouldn't forgive a small sum. But I had no idea that the ten thousand talents owed by the wicked servant was equivalent to tens of thousands of *years'* worth of wages. I completely missed the severity of the debt in the parable because no one had ever explained that the balance due was around a billion American dollars!

After delivering this parable, Jesus also shared that Father God would not forgive us if we chose not to forgive. Ouch.

Even with some understanding of that parable, however, for the majority of my life I typically responded to forgiveness recommendations with indignant scoffing.

"They don't deserve forgiveness! Look at the offense and harm that was done to me! Forgiving them means they get away with it, and how is that fair? *What about ME?!* I will never forgive that!"

Jesus needed to write his truth from the seventh chapter of the book of Luke onto my heart for my mind and my will to receive it. "Therefore I tell you, her sins, which are many, are forgiven—for she loved much. But he who is forgiven little, loves little" (ESV Luke 7:47). In order to receive that, I had to choose to lay down my stubborn, rebellious will.

Cyndi's voice was always wise and tender as she discipled me into understanding. "Forgiveness is not a feeling, honey. Forgiveness is a decision made in obedience to the Lord, out of the awareness of everything he has forgiven you for."

My mentor sat across from me in one of many inner healing prayer sessions. On the couch in her cozy study with its library wall full of books and Cyndi relaxing in her overstuffed wingback, I felt like a teenager having a heart-to-heart talk with her favorite aunt. It was a safe place to be authentic.

Oh, how I despised that word. *Obedience.* It's probably one of the top three commands decreed by every good Southern Baptist preacher, parent, and Sunday School teacher worldwide. Hefty black King James Bible held aloft with one hand, while the other hand pointed a finger in my face as the holder boomed, "You WILL obey!"

It's interesting that Jesus didn't ever do that.

The word *obedience* often elicited a visceral response down into my very being. Rage. Dishonor. Terror. Shame. Guilt. And so much injustice. All mashed together with nowhere to go.

But as the Lord began to woo me back to himself with the kind of tenderness that only he can convey, I began to understand a totally new definition of obedience. Reverence. Safety. Gratitude. Honor. Peace. And so much love. All mashed together into a highly desirable and rewarding treasure.

Cyndi continued to lead me.

"I want you to close your eyes and picture an empty chair, and I want you to imagine your mom sitting in that chair."

I saw the picture in my mind's eye, and all the feelings came. Rage. Voicelessness. Resentment. Grief.

Cyndi coached me gently. "And remembering that forgiveness isn't a feeling but it's a choice, I'm going to ask you to repeat out loud after me. Ready?"

I took a deep breath. "Ready."

She spoke softly. "'Mom, I choose to forgive you.' Now, you say that back to me out loud, but imagine you're saying it to her directly."

I took another deep breath as I started to repeat. "Mom . . ." Hot tears threatened, my voice cracking.

"Mom, I choose . . ." I cleared my throat to force the words. "Mom, I choose to forgive you."

She continued leading. "For every way you couldn't be the mom I needed or deserved."

I exhaled the words as it felt like a flood was leaving my body along with them. I continued to repeat after Cyndi through heavy tears.

"Mom, I forgive you, for not being emotionally connected to me. I forgive you for being such an angry mom, and for every time you yelled. Mom, I forgive you for not protecting me from Uncle Jack, for blaming me and Dad for what Jack did, and for choosing to do nothing about the abuse. This dishonored me, and I didn't deserve it. And I forgive you for the effects this has had on my life.

"Mom, I forgive you for every pity party, for always favoring Edgar, and for judging and criticizing me. I forgive that you were so hard to please, and that it seemed like everything was always about you. I forgive you for needing to be the center of attention, and for pouting when you weren't."

On and on we went until I had forgiven every infraction on Cyndi's lengthy list that we had identified. The more I forgave, the lighter I became. Decades of heaviness, injustice, and rage just melted away as the darkness in my heart gave way to light. Many good, healthy tears fell. Until this day, I had never known the concept of beneficial, cleansing tears. These weren't the signs of weakness or emotional hysteria that I had known them to be. They were a necessary part of releasing and acknowledging the very real pain and grief I had bottled up for most of my life. This experience was profound.

Three days after this first session of prayer with Cyndi, I went by Mom's house for an obligatory short visit. The moment I saw her, I realized that something supernatural had happened. All the usual irritation, frustration, and disdain that I had typically felt in her presence was simply gone. I could see her from a completely new perspective, and her capacity to continue to hurt me had vanished. It almost felt as if we were different people.

She had not changed. I had.

And whatever all of that was, I wanted much more.

Lord, I forgive myself that it took me over forty-five years to forgive my mom. I forgive her for being so hard to forgive and for every negative effect she had on my life. I repent for holding onto resentment and bitterness. I choose not to hold onto these any longer, and I release it all to you, Jesus. Amen.

Chapter Twenty-Five
INIQUITY

"Is someone in your family involved in the Freemasons?"

The tiny but powerful lady with mousy gray hair and bright blue eyes withdrew her hands from me as if I were a leper with Covid. She wasn't angry at me, but her eyes were wide. Only a moment before, she had laid her hands on my forearms to pray for me as we sat in the prayer room at the back of our church. She had flinched as soon as she touched me.

I felt something like national pride rise up in me as I answered.

"Oh yes! My grandfather was a thirty-third degree Mason, and my great-grandmother was a High Priestess in the Order of the Eastern Star."

Her expression changed, and my rising pride plummeted.

"You may want to do some digging on that. It's much darker than anyone realizes. I could actually feel it on you when I touched you."

Part of me thought she was being ridiculous and dramatic. Who says things like that? The other part of me was deeply curious.

Cyndi recommended several things for me to read, and I was grieved and shocked at what I learned. I read about the spoken vows and curses that every member of the Masonic utters aloud as part of their rituals. I learned that many of those spoken curses intentionally call forth evil onto their own offspring, and that the "brothers" vow to esteem their members above all others, even in matters of law and justice. I discovered that supernatural levels of power and control are part of the draw that attracts young men into the order, and my eyes were opened to many other heinous truths about the Masonic that the average person knows nothing about.

I wept hard as I read aloud a prayer that had been recommended to me to deal with the issue of having Freemasons in my ancestry.

"I renounce the Hoodwink blindfold, and its effects on the spirit, emotions, and eyes; including all confusion, fear of the dark, fear of the light, and fear of sudden noises."[1]

I almost couldn't continue as many of the puzzle pieces of my life slammed together in revelation.

For the entirety of my life, even into my forties, I had been afflicted by a fear of sudden noises. Every clap of thunder, every blast of fireworks on the Fourth of July, and every rusty old car that backfired on the road sent me into a quick but profound moment of absolute terror. My heart would race, my skin would prickle and flush, and I would shudder. It usually took me several minutes to calm down.

I had also forever been petrified of the dark.

I remember sitting on the potty just after midnight without the light on. I didn't want the sasquatch ceiling fan to wake up and eat me. My eight-year-old heart was terrified, and I thought I saw roaches crawling all over the wall.

Actually, there were no roaches. My parents hadn't yet discovered that I desperately needed glasses to see, and what I saw as roaches were just the flower clusters on the bathroom wallpaper. But in that moment, those miniature rosebuds were a legion of disgusting insects in formation just waiting to crawl all over me.

My crying must have awakened my mom because she knocked softly on the door. As she opened it, a tiny bit of the glow from the hall nightlight brought just enough visibility into the bathroom for me to see Mom hand me a Nutter Butter cookie and walk away.

I felt sad and surprisingly pitied at the same time. Pitied because Mom had actually tried to show me a rare measure of comfort. Sad because she never asked me what the matter was, because she didn't stay, and because she had no idea how much I hated Nutter Butters.

I was so surprised at her act of kindness that I ate the

cookie anyway. That, plus the slight increase of light through the open door, was enough to settle my scared little heart so that I could go back to bed. But the demons lurking in darkness were still my companions for many years.

A study of the Hebrew origins of Scripture reveals that iniquity is the generational sin mentioned within the Ten Commandments, which passes down to the grandchildren for up to four generations. There was no framework for this truth in our Baptist doctrine. But in my mid-forties as I read through that prayer of release and renunciation of the Masonic and its curses, I could physically feel the fears leaving me as decades of micro traumas melted away. For the first time in my life, I knew that I was free of that fear.

After I realized the effects of my prayer, I knew I needed to share my revelations with the family. I was surprised that I didn't receive pushback from Mom and Dad given their ages and cultural norms. But they readily accepted the truth about the need to address the generational wrongs. So we held a family meeting in their living room with all five of us as Dad somberly read aloud the lengthy prayer of renunciation of Freemasonry.

Something shifted in their home that day. We all shed tears of grief and repentance as we took ownership of the things entered into by our ancestors. We also felt the heavy spiritual impact of our prayers in the natural realm. A few times the walls themselves actually shook and at least a few picture frames crashed to the floor. We were touching heaven, and the environment knew it.

And I can now enjoy fireworks because I have never been the same.

Lord, I choose to forgive and release my ancestors for their involvement in the Freemasons. I forgive every curse and vow they spoke, and I forgive them for what this brought into our family. I renounce all involvement with the Freemasons and I break agreement with their power in my bloodline. I forgive Mom for her lack of comfort and for not asking questions when I was scared. I release it all to you, Jesus. Amen.

Chapter Twenty-Six
CLEAN

"The Word of God says that Jesus will never leave us or forsake us. He is always there, Nanci. We just have to look for where he was."

Cyndi sat with me talking about Scripture as I had never heard it before. It wasn't theoretical or symbolic. Jesus actually meant what he said.

Anger sparked briefly.

"So if Jesus is always there, why didn't he stop it?"

Cyndi smiled softly.

"We live in a fallen world, sweetie," she answered. "Sin and decay and death came in at the garden, and the enemy has been destroying people ever since. God gave all of humanity free will, and out of that free will, people do horrible things that grieve the heart of God. Jesus called satan the ruler of this world. And remember what Jesus said about trouble? He said in this world we would absolutely have trouble. But then he said to take heart because he had overcome the world."

Opening the door of the most heavily guarded room in my heart was a dangerous act that I had never planned to do. But in the light of the presence of Jesus himself, my aversion dissipated. Soft tears fell, and an ache in my heart began to form as the memory came into focus on the movie screen of my mind.

I was barely three years old, and a musty sheet covered me completely so I couldn't see. I was in my great-uncle's bed, and I felt the painful loss of my innocence. The swirl of emotions was hard. Injustice. Confusion. Powerlessness. Fear. Grief. Shame. Dirty.

"Nanci, I want you to ask this question out loud. Jesus, can you show me where you were?"

I hadn't finished praying half of the prayer before deep, heaving sobs erupted. In the movie screen of my mind, I very clearly saw Jesus as a visible person, standing between the door and the bed. He looked with anger at the violation taking place, and then he wept in grief over what had been stolen.

I was undone. It was hard to find a place to put the tangible awareness of the presence of Jesus in the midst of my trauma, and the revelation of the pain he felt for me was a supernatural balm.

My savior grieved. For me. And Cyndi was right: he had never left me.

In my mind's eye, the next scenes moved in a flash.

Jesus beckoned my mother into the room, and she came in (just as she had done in real life), and the abuse stopped. Then I saw Jesus sit down on the edge of the defiled bed, and he cradled me in his lap after placing a clean, white nightgown on my exposed body.

As Cyndi led me in identifying and releasing every emotion out loud one by one to the Lord, he took every one of those feelings I had buried for decades and replaced them with cleanliness, purity, and peace. Then she led me in several prayers of forgiveness and release of Uncle Jack, my grandparents, and my parents who had not protected me nor done anything in my defense. In the safe, loving lap of Jesus, this came easily.

Healing phrases from the heart of Jesus flowed through my mind.

"It wasn't your fault. You didn't deserve this. This wasn't my Father's will for you. This does not define you. This is not who you are."

A heaviness I had never known I was carrying melted away as I wept and rocked in the arms of my Savior. He gave me a garment of praise for the spirit of heaviness. He washed me and made me whiter than snow.

I am clean.

Lord, I choose to forgive Uncle Jack for violating me and stealing my innocence at such an early age. I forgive him for the effects that this had on my life. I forgive my parents for not protecting me, and I forgive my mom for making me believe it was my fault. I release all of the shame, the dishonor, the trauma, and the fear to you, Lord, and I receive your healing and your cleansing. In your holy name, amen.

Chapter Twenty-Seven
HEIGHTS

My fingernails almost drew blood as I gripped Brian's shoulders in front of me. We descended all 219 steps of the Saint Augustine lighthouse at a slower-than-snail's pace so I wouldn't pass out from my panic. I was in my forties, and I was a pitiable sight.

I had been terrified of heights for as long as I could remember. Even if I wasn't the one up high, like while watching Edgar and Jillian scamper across a rope bridge or seeing a random kid climb a random tree, terror would grip me. My mind played out the absolute worst outcomes in full color. These images were always filled with crushed brains, bones snapped and protruding, and epic amounts of blood.

This fear really detracted from my ability to enjoy things like state parks with rock formations created to be hiked, and touristy places like Niagara Falls and the Empire State Building. More than a few times, I tried to force myself into courage and take a step or two toward the scary precipice. Without fail, even when there was a reinforced steel barricade between me and death, my body would respond to the threat, and I would involuntarily collapse in a tearful, trembling heap.

Somehow I neglected to calculate my exit plan when visiting the lighthouse. Going up was beautiful and breezy. But the fact that the steps were ornately designed ironwork stairs with open grating and visibility all 175 feet down had escaped me, until I hit the top stair and had to turn around. Like the elongation of the murderous hotel hall splashed with r-e-d-r-u-m in *The Shining*, that staircase yawned and opened straight into the eternal pit of darkness. Hence my death grip on my patient husband as he helped me navigate down to safety.

Growing up, Mom was never kind or tender in the face of my phobia. I don't think she ever once asked me if I was afraid. She would just roll her eyes at my crying and leave me there to get it together. Sometimes she would even join my brother and sister on whatever high adventure they were enjoying, leaving me to hold her purse and her Pall Malls alone.

It never once entered my head that this kind of fear could actually be healed.

"So the way you start to heal a past trauma is to invite Jesus into it," the guest speaker shared from the pulpit.

"Malachi 4:2 says that the sun of righteousness will arise with healing in its wings. That word *wings* there also means 'corners' in Hebrew, as in the flowing corner tassels of the garment Jesus wore. He is our sun of righteousness with healing in his wings."

The visiting presenter who was teaching at what she called a "healing prayer workshop" was sharing applications of Scripture like no one I had ever heard before. This minister, Monte Bromiley, the founder of Beth Shalom Ministries of Texas, had spent over thirty years praying individually with thousands of hurting and broken people. Through training, trial and error, and spending time under powerfully anointed mentors, she had developed a prayer process that, in a single long session, addressed the majority of the emotional and spiritual baggage most people carry.

I learned that open doors like sin and lies and trauma were avenues for the enemy to plant his seeds in us, and this speaker taught that we could pray for those seeds and their negative effects to be erased when we invite Jesus into that issue on purpose. Monte challenged all of us in attendance that anyone who follows the Lord Jesus could pray with people this way. I wasn't too sure that just anyone could pray like this; it seemed to me some people were just anointed with this gifting. But her arguments were compelling, and she also encouraged us that we could pray this way for our own issues.

So I decided a few days later to test out the theories

Monte taught. I sat with a legal pad and pen, snuggled under my bed covers, and I asked the Lord to bring any trauma to mind that needed healing. A memory from age six surfaced immediately.

"What do you mean, you hit your head?!" Mom barked. "I just got back from the emergency room with Jillian!"

Mom was enraged, again. My sister and I had been jumping from her top bunk to our dresser to the floor and back up again. Like our own personal roller coaster, round and round we went. We would launch ourselves from the corner of the top bunk, sail the two feet between the bed and the dresser, then jump down from the dresser onto a pillow on the floor. While my feet were hitting the pillow, Jillian's feet were leaping from the bed. We made it into a race to see who could catch the other.

Until Jillian went wrong and caught her head on the edge of the dresser. Lots of blood and yelling and a few stitches later, she and I were back at the roller coaster jumping. Then I was the one who went wrong, and it was my turn for stitches. My feet had slipped as I landed on the dresser, and the back of my skull caught the sharp, wooden corner of the slightly ajar dresser drawer that never closed properly. My head gash was in exactly the same spot as Jillian's.

I had always seen this event as a normal childhood boo-boo and nothing more.

Incorporating the tools I had learned in Monte's

healing prayer workshop, I allowed the memory of the injury to play like a movie in my mind as I asked Jesus to show me where he was.

I smiled as I saw Jesus pick me up from the floor just after I had fallen and hit my head. He touched the open gash gently with one hand and kissed me on the forehead. Then he lifted me up in his hands and placed me back up on top of the bunkbed. Then the movie ended. It made no sense to me why Jesus had done that, but I just chalked it up to mystery and let it go.

Three days later, I discovered why Jesus had done what he had done.

Brian and I had taken a detour out to the Grand Canyon after a business trip, and we were able to arrive at the canyon rim just before the blue-black of dawn. Aware of my tendency to be terrified of heights, we nestled with flashlights amongst a growing crowd well away from the ledge but close enough to feel the buffeting winds.

Everyone should experience the Grand Canyon for the first time along with the sunrise. As the first hints of light begin to creep in, the blackened landscape starts to take on uniform hues of muted grayish brown. Then as the light increases, dusky uniformity gives way to orange and rust and every other shade as each ledge and crevice becomes recognizable. It's like standing behind the artist as he adds more paint to the canvas.

As the sun crested the horizon, we all stood with our blankets draped over us to stare at the overwhelming beauty beneath. The entire crowd was completely silent at the sight. It felt like the noise of conversation would ruin it. Along with the others nearby, we inched closer to the ledge to get a better look. I dug my fingers into Brian's arm expecting the usual hyperventilation and involuntary tremors to spoil the moment. But my sense of overwhelm turned from external to internal, and I marveled at my complete lack of fear.

I had been totally healed and delivered of my fear of heights without even asking. Jesus had known where the phobia had begun, and by placing me back up on that bunk bed, he had permanently erased the fear. My body changed from that encounter with Jesus, and I no longer have to miss out on the heights.

Lord, I thank you for making my feet like those of a deer, and for setting me up on my high places as it's written in the second book of Samuel. I forgive my mom for her annoyance at my injury and at my fear of heights, and I forgive my body for partnering with that fear. Lord, I rejoice in the healing you orchestrated. In your holy name, amen.

Chapter Twenty-Eight
GRACE

Apparently I was supposed to be a tumor. Prenatal sonograms weren't commonplace in the mid-1960s. So if multiples were suspected, doctors relied upon external abdominal exams and the detection of heartbeats. The size and shape of Mom's belly clearly indicated more than one little bundle of joy in there. But at checkup after checkup, there was only one really strong heartbeat found.

To add to the evidence, Mom had experienced some brief but severe cramping and unusual bleeding around gestational month six. So doctors concluded that there must be a tumor growing alongside the baby, and they told Mom they would sort it all out at the delivery.

I can only imagine my mom's shock when a second heartbeat was detected forty-eight hours before she went into labor. So she was sent for an X-ray, and sure enough, there I was.

I suppose the lack of time to prepare for my arrival should explain why Mom had no name chosen for me. She had decided before she was in second grade that the name of her first daughter must be Jillian. Mom told many stories about naming all of her dolls Jillian after hearing the name on a television program and just loving the sound of it. Jillian was born first, so she received the sacred name. Two minutes later, Twin B came along.

Twins and triplets and other multiples understand the unique and not always pleasant perspective of birth names and identities. Most singly born children have never considered the position of being an afterthought, or an "uh oh, there's another one." We hear the dreamy stories our parents tell of planning and longing for their child, and we sense all the favor and blessing our parents intended to bestow. But those blessings typically belong to the firstborn, not to Twin B. It seemed my parents always thought the "surprised by twins" stories were cute. As Twin B, I didn't think they were cute at all.

Mom chose to name me after whichever one of her many sisters showed up at the hospital to visit first. Turns out that her first family visitor was her little sister Nancy. Except Mom wanted my name to be different. So she spelled it Nanci.

Unusually spelled names are all well and good until everyone but you can find your name monogrammed on a souvenir or a bedroom door sign spelled as you spell it. Still to this day, most people misspell my name, even when it's visibly written right in front of them and they have known me for years.

I hated my name from as early as I can recall. I very much liked my Aunt after whom I was named. But people would shorten my name to all sorts of things I didn't care for. Nan. Nannygoat. NannerNanner. *Ugh.* And to make it worse, another aunt in Mom's family decided to also name her first daughter Nancy (spelled commonly). So now there were three Nancys in the room at every family gathering.

Several of my many aunts, uncles, and cousins decided to differentiate by just referring to me and Jillian as "the twins" as if we were a single unit. We had already been forced to share birthday cakes and bathtub time and clothes. Why not share identities as well? Grandmother actually referred to us several times as "whichever." It made no difference to her. There's a special kind of hurt that lodges into the heart of a child when her very own grandmother doesn't care to get her name right.

I often daydreamed about legally changing my name to something exotic like Darcy or Layla or Crystal. Those girls never had to share their birthday cakes with anyone, and they could always find their names on souvenirs.

I was forty-seven years old before I understood the beauty and sacredness of my name.

Spending time in prayer one day in the season when I

was learning how to hear and see Jesus with the eyes of my heart, he showed me something just after I had read, again, that my name means "Grace of God." In the movie screen of my mind, Jesus walked me to a white door and opened it. He said, "This is the room I have prepared for you in my Father's mansion."

The door swung open to reveal a bedroom that I could not have designed more perfectly. It was all white. White farmhouse walls, white wrought-iron bed with a white country eyelet lace comforter, and rustic white country furniture. Curled up at the foot of this bed lay my cat that had died the month before, and on the white desk in front of a window there was a white vase with yellow jonquils in it. My favorite flower. The room was all me, and it was so lovely.

I wept softly as I saw a single word painted in multiple colors on the wall over the bed in huge cursive script.

"Grace."

I have cherished my name since.

Lord, I repent for despising the name I was given, and I forgive myself for that. I forgive the doctors who labeled me a tumor. I forgive Mom for favoring Jillian's name over mine, and I forgive her for how the unusual spelling of my name has affected my life. I thank you, Lord, for showing me how you see my name, and for teaching me to cherish it. In your holy name, amen.

Chapter Twenty-Nine
NOT MY CIRCUS

My mother loved a live professional circus. Whether it was the traveling big top tent with dancing elephants or the shows at the local theme park with death-defying acrobats, she would grin like a kid on Christmas morning at the organized chaos.

She also seemed to love creating circus-like conditions for everyone around her.

As best as I could tell, Mom needed to create trouble for others in order to deflect any attention to her poor decisions. Igniting strife and conflict between others is a pretty effective shield. It was also quite the source of irritation. I have growled audibly many times at Mom's behavior.

Triangulation was one of her favorite tools. After a long phone call with Jillian, Mom would promptly phone me to report on a few juicy tidbits from Jillian's life, but she would twist them ever so slightly to create drama. If Jillian's son was doing well in football, Mom would color the story as if Jillian were declaring her son to have much more athletic skill and talent than my son. I knew Jillian would never make such a comment, but it would usually ruin my afternoon as I played over the words in my mind and wondered if the insult might be true.

After my visits with Mom, she would immediately call Jillian to spin the things I had shared. If Brian was becoming dissatisfied with his job and he was considering a move, she would report to Jillian that Brian wasn't being mindful of his obligations to provide, and she feared we might end up in the poor house. The truth was actually the polar opposite. So when Jillian would relay Mom's comments back to me, it would trigger my defensiveness and once again ruin my afternoon.

Several times Mom even had the audacity to compare our children to us directly.

I remember one conversation where she sighed deeply on the other end of the phone. "You know I'm just not sure that Jillian is doing as much with her kids spiritually as you and Brian are. She and Brad seem to be all about the education. I mean, don't get me wrong, her kids are the smartest kids I've ever seen, even smarter than yours. And yes, education is important. But I'm really worried that she isn't giving them a good Christian foundation."

Um. Thanks?

After comparing notes, Jillian and I discovered that

Mom had remarked to Jillian about my kids the very same afternoon. "I'm just so proud of how brilliant your kids are! I just don't think Nanci cares very much about educating her kids like you do. I mean, don't get me wrong, her kids are really focused on their faith, they're way more spiritually grounded than your kids are, and of course that's important. But I'm really worried that she isn't giving them a good educational foundation."

Thanks again?

There isn't really a good response to back-door insults like these. I tried not to let the comments hurt me, but I would be lying if I didn't admit they often stung.

When she would make comments about the things my sister-in-law Wendy had supposedly said about hating me and disapproving of my personal decisions, Mom was looking for a fight to erupt between me and Wendy. She enjoyed seeing this kind of drama the way drivers enjoy staring like rubberneckers at a traffic accident on the other side of the road. She loved making subtle comments full of negativity and judgment, and she was looking to sow discord and watch the ensuing battle.

She began many conversations with questions such as, "Do you know what Wendy said about you last week?" Or "You know, Edgar thinks that what you and Brian are doing at church is heresy, and he doesn't see how you can be talking to others about Jesus when you weren't a great sister to him." Any response I gave would be taken straight back to the original offender. So I could either erupt in a verbal tirade that would be twisted about me later, or I could keep my mouth shut and seethe.

Her most effective method of stirring up conflict was to drop these hints with each of us individually just before we were scheduled to gather for a big family meal. She knew that everyone would walk in hating the other guests, and she would watch everyone's faces for reactions as she sweetly passed the gravy.

I worked hard at trying to let these things go, but many times I would find myself playing the mental game where I waged long, involved arguments in my head with the offender. I would devise the perfect retort to Wendy or Edgar in my mind and deliver a beautiful defense, all the while growing more offended. This kind of spiraling is pointless and exhausting, but I did it often.

Over time I began to wise up enough not to take her bait. I learned to be more aware of her motives and her tendency to make things up, so I chose not to believe most of what she said. If there was some shred of truth to her statement, I began to choose to give the other person the benefit of the doubt. I would still huff and roll my eyes in annoyance toward Mom, but this maturing on my part was a step in the right direction.

But Edgar and Wendy never figured Mom out. They believed absolutely everything she said, and in their emotional immaturity, they were incapable of simply letting it go as I did. It still pricked at my heart though.

Then in a conversation with my brother-in-law Brad,

he used a phrase that I'd never heard before. He was unfazed by my mother, and he explained how that was possible. "When I look at her, I just think, 'Not my circus, not my monkeys.'" What a liberating concept!

Mom's need to foster divisive chaos was producing a circus, and her negative comments were her monkeys. It turns out that whenever she presented her circus, I had a choice. I could choose not to step inside the ring. It was profoundly freeing for me to receive the truth that I am not required to take one ounce of responsibility for the drama and chaos that anyone else wants to stir up.

That statement also gave me permission to no longer take my mother's comments personally. I came to the truth that her perspective of me was self-centered and unrelated to who I am.

It had nothing to do with me.

When I really thought about it, I clearly understood I was unlikely to ever receive my mother's approval. She had made that fairly clear to me as a child and a young adult. Looking at this awareness through the lens of circuses and monkeys, I began to realize that my mother simply did not have the capacity to honor or unconditionally accept others. There wasn't a loving well out of which to speak kindly. It simply wasn't there. So instead of my sitting in frustration and offense because she couldn't be kind or positive, I could choose to accept that grace was a language she wasn't taught to speak.

This took a lot of pressure off my expectations for her.

When I began to change my expectations that she would ever learn how to speak the language of kindness and grace, I found myself much less angry and offended by her typical behavior. I no longer dreaded my visits with her.

I suppose it's somewhat similar to the expectations we have of a person who was born blind. They didn't wish to be born blind. It wasn't their plan. So we don't become angry at the blind person when they bump into something. We don't become offended when they can't tell us what color the sky is today or whether a paint swatch matches the sofa pattern. If we have even the tiniest shred of humanity, we accept gracefully that the blind cannot do these things. There is zero judgment.

When I began to look at my mother with an awareness of what she would likely never have, I stopped judging her, and I stopped waiting for it. That release of expectation brought great freedom. It became easy for me to walk into her house grounded in my own peace and joy, and those remained with me throughout my visit. No longer would my peace be robbed from me. It also resulted in my not being surprised when she behaved in her typical unkind manner. And on the few times when she did exhibit grace and kindness, I could be pleasantly surprised at the rare display.

As I began to lay down my expectations of her ever changing, something supernatural and unexpected seemed to occur. In many ways, she did become kinder and less negative.

Perhaps there's much more to the spiritual realm than we often consider. I have read elsewhere that forgiveness causes a chain reaction in the heavens. So perhaps through my release of judgment and my decision to choose love despite bad behavior, something spiritually shifted within Mom that freed her up to allow love to flow more easily.

When both of us are free, no one needs a circus.

Lord Jesus, I forgive my mom for her need to stir up chaos and division. I forgive her for every time she presented her circus and her monkeys, and for never learning how to speak the language of grace. I forgive her mother for failing to pass on unconditional love, and I repent for the many years that I carried offense. I let it all go, and I thank you, Lord, for releasing me. In your holy name, amen.

Chapter Thirty
REAL

"Well," I started. "I'm getting the picture in my mind of an old, naked, plastic baby doll lying discarded in a corner on the floor, but that makes no sense."

I sat on the sofa across from Shelly, an inner healing prayer minister that Cyndi had recommended. Using the Beth Shalom model of healing prayer that she had learned from Monte Bromiley, Shelly had just inventoried every trauma and wounding from my entire life. Through a two-hour interview, she had recorded a timeline that contained every incident from the moment of my conception up until recent weeks. We left nothing out.

In this ministry process, Shelly had asked the Lord to give me a mental picture of what it was like deep within the core of my innermost self, in that innermost place that David wrote about in Psalm 51. Immediately the image of the plastic 1970s Baby Tender Love doll formed in my thoughts. The doll was on the floor under a baby crib as if it had been dropped there. Confused, I described what I had seen to Shelly.

She smiled. "Of course! It's fake. It's plastic. It isn't real. You had to be fake and plastic your whole life! It's the only way you were able to survive. You were forced to put on a front to hide all of the abuse. That discarded plastic doll is you."

Ugly crying erupted as I resonated with every word she said. There had been no setting in my childhood where it had been safe for me to be real.

Guided by the Holy Spirit, Shelly led me to repeat after her in prayer.

"Lord Jesus, I invite you into this innermost part of me. Your Word says that if we invite you in, you will come in. I don't want to be fake! Just like Pinocchio, I want to be real. Jesus, come and make me real."

The visual of Baby Tender Love disappeared and a new vision of the Lord took its place in my mind's eye. Walking up to me as a screaming infant in a crib, Jesus picked me up and held me to his chest. The infant version of myself immediately settled down and fell asleep.

When I saw this image of Jesus holding me close up to his chest and cradling my little head in his big hand, I realized that my mom had never held me this way. In every photo of my infancy, if I wasn't propped up in an infant seat or crawling around in a playpen, Mom was holding me in the crook of her elbow with me facing outward. She would be engaged with a task or making conversation with anyone but the baby in her arms. Being held by her was never an intimate embrace. Many tears fell.

Shelly had me thank Jesus for making me real, and we asked him to walk with me through all the places in my heart we needed to go.

With Shelly's leading, I forgave everything related to Mom: her revisionist history, her drama, her ignoring of the abuse and blaming me. I even forgave my grandmother for labeling Mom as the black sheep of the family.

As I forgave this, the Lord brought to my mind that picture of Grandmother's yarn art wall piece that showed the one black sheep representing my mom amidst all of the white sheep. In the movie screen of my mind, Jesus walked up to that artwork and painted over the black sheep with his blood, and I watched in wonder as the black sheep turned white like the rest.

I continued to follow Shelly's leading and forgive all of the generational baggage and bloodline sin on both sides of my family. As I did this, the image of the infant me that Jesus was holding began to change. I started to get older and bigger. Like a time lapse in a movie reel that shows a character quickly aging through scene after scene, I watched the chronology. Jesus held me as a toddler, then laughed with me as a preschooler. The more I forgave and released and renounced, the more the image of me grew and matured.

As Shelly and I neared the end of the long list of things to forgive and release, the image in my mind's eye was of me around five years old. The me that I saw was a pretty little girl. I noticed this because I had never heard nor believed I was pretty. I felt rather ugly as a child, but this little girl was definitely not ugly.

I stood close to Jesus, holding his hand as he walked me through my childhood home where all of the trauma and wounding had taken place. Jesus opened every single door to every single room in that house. Growing up there, it had always felt dark and dirty. Now with Jesus, the rooms were all empty, clean and swept, light and airy.

After we walked out the front door together, he knelt down and picked me up and propped me on his hip.

He looked me in the eye and grinned as he said, "I would love to introduce you to someone and show you off. Let's go say hi to my Father."

He is real. And so am I.

Mom and Dad, I choose to forgive you both for the ways that you were fake and for creating an environment where I had to be fake. I forgive that it wasn't safe for me to be real. Lord, I praise and thank you for healing my identity, for making me real, and for sweeping my house clean. In your holy name, amen.

Chapter Thirty-One
HOLY ANGUISH

As I moved to leave Cyndi's house one afternoon, I stopped for a moment. "You know, it's really starting to bother me that I don't like people very much. Like, I'm not a very nice person. I just don't care about anybody except Brian and the kids."

We had just spent some sweet prayer time together, and I made this comment in passing as I headed out to my next errand. I was starting to become aware of my hatred of other people the closer I grew to the Lord, and I began to feel convicted by the condition of my heart.

For most of my adult life, I was not a nice person. To their faces I would be professional and polite to people, but I saw them as an annoying intrusion at best, and as worthless morons at worst. I had zero interest in making conversation with strangers in an elevator, greeting people at church, or caring if a harried mother in the checkout line ahead of me was three dollars short with her grocery purchase. Where others might feel kindness or connection, I felt standoffish and irritated.

In my decades-long career in human resources, I judged, condemned, and word-cursed thousands of people in my heart as I rolled my eyes at typos on a resume or snickered at a candidate's mismatched clothing. My haughty, air-sniffing manner wasn't necessarily evident to others. But I embraced it internally.

I never considered that the practices of judgment and criticism prevalent in Mom's family, which had been passed along to me, were in any way problematic or wrong. I can still see Grandmother staring down her nose with a scowl as she watched a passing restaurant server whose skirt was too skimpy. She never tried to hold back her judgy comment about what the good Lord's world was coming to. There was not an ounce of warmth or grace or compassion in Grandmother, and she made sure to loudly explain what was inappropriate about all of the mongrels who passed us by. She made it easy to join in.

She often looked down her nose at my mother, her middle daughter, as well. Mom was the only one of her siblings not to complete her college degree. This was apparently quite a black mark upon the family. My grandmother also greatly disliked my father from the beginning, and she made sure Mom knew this. Moments before walking down the wedding ceremony aisle, Grandmother whispered into my mother's ear, "I'm convinced this is a mistake and it won't work out. You can come back home whenever that happens." There was nothing my mother could do to be liked, or truly loved, by her mother.

Mom spent plenty of her own time commenting about all that was inappropriate in others and making sure she taught her children that such swill were separate and not like us. This was all behind their backs, of course. A good Christian doesn't insult a person to their face. It's no wonder I became the jerk of a person I was with examples like these.

Apparently the Lord was just waiting for me to give him an open door, and the confession to Cyndi was the door he needed.

A few weeks after sharing that comment with Cyndi, Brian and I had taken a camping trip into the nearby hills where we did little else but rest, pray, and worship in the woods. As we drove back home along winding rural roads dotted with poor country shacks, the Lord invaded the car. An open vision unrolled as I looked at those passing, ragged homes. Their walls and porches disappeared, and I could see the people inside. What I saw broke me.

Inside every home, I saw people crying out, weeping, on their knees begging the Lord to bring peace and freedom. These people knew the Lord, but their hearts were broken with grief and trauma, and they had no one to help them. I could feel their desperate pain and hear the sound of their cries.

Undone, I erupted into heaving sobs and had to ask Brian to pull the car over. My heart was grieved for these hurting people in a way I could barely comprehend, and the weight of this heartbreak brought physical pain to my chest. I understood clearly that the Lord was breaking my heart for what breaks his heart.

In that moment, I received a supernatural love for people. Humanity has never looked the same since.

Several years after this experience, I was finally able to place a label on what had happened. In the introduction of a book written by evangelist John Ramirez, the author recalls a moment when the Lord had broken his heart in a similar way. John labeled it a baptism of holy anguish[1].

My heart leaped as I read the phrase. That was it! That was what the Lord had so graciously done for me. He had given me his heart for his people, and I had no idea what he had in store as a result.

Lord, I forgive Grandmother for her pride and critical judgment of others. I forgive her for passing that onto my mother, and I forgive my mom for teaching that to me. I repent for walking in judgment and hatred of people, and I forgive myself. I renounce judgment and pride, and Lord, I receive your love for others in exchange. In your holy name, amen.

Chapter Thirty-Two
DISCOVERING DESTINY

"You mean you quit your job?" Mom looked incredulous. "How in the world are you going to provide for yourself?!"

She looked around at the simply furnished prayer ministry office that Brian and I had just set up in our small, finished basement. I had resigned from my twenty-five-year corporate human resources career at the Lord's very clear leading through dreams and divine appointments, and I had surrendered to full-time, unpaid, Christian ministry. I knew this was my calling.

Mom's concept of destiny was to build a secure and predictable future by forced labor and grinding effort. She was convinced that any modern woman needed to have her own checking accounts, her own retirement plans, and an admirable credit score. In her mind, a woman must always be prepared to provide for herself. She had no grid for tangible, supernatural provision from God in real life.

She had also never considered that a husband can be the sole financial provider for a household. Not a single family within her circle of community had a wife who did not work outside the home full-time, including all of her siblings and church friends. The concept was foreign, and in her eyes, foolish.

My response bounced off her deeply legalistic framework with a thud.

"We just know this is what God has told us to do. We're at total peace about it."

It saddened me that she could only shrug and change the subject, because I was never able to share the revelation of my destiny with her.

About eight months prior to this, I had experienced powerful encounters with the Lord through times of healing ministry with Cyndi. She would lead me through various kinds of listening or reflective prayer, and she taught me how to trust the still, small voice of the Lord with the ears of my heart.

Through those prayers, I had begun to press in hard to learn more about the healing of my wounds and lies. The Lord had been wrecking and refining my heart, pulling down all kinds of belief systems and habits of pride and criticism. Amidst all of this glorious unraveling, the Lord began to press upon me to act on his behalf with strangers. I would walk past an elderly man alone in the produce aisle or a woman in a wheelchair at the grocery checkout line, and I would feel the Holy Spirit nudge me. In my mind's eye, he would give me a quick impression of praying for them or blessing them financially, and he was teaching me how to hear and respond in obedience to his promptings despite my fear of looking like an idiot.

In seeing God touch these people through my willingness, while I was also studying many prayer training materials during every free moment, a faith began to rise up in me. I began to envision myself being able to minister to others for the healing of their wounds and lies. I embraced the possibility that I might just be able to pray one-on-one with people the way Cyndi and Shelly had prayed with me. It felt terrifying and exciting.

Just a few months into my immersive studying season, the Lord orchestrated a divine appointment for my husband and me. As the summer season was winding down, we found ourselves at an outdoor church for the homeless at a public park near Daytona Beach. I knew it was the Lord because up until this season I had carried a hypercritical disdain for the homeless and the poor and addicted. My religious spirit judged these outcasts to be pitiful victims of their own sinful choices, most undeserving of compassion or grace. But as I stepped toward this ragtag group near the beach, all I felt was love as I heard the Lord say, "This is my church, and this is good."

The ocean breeze tempered the already sweltering

Florida sun, as palm trees and sea oats rustled in the wind. My heart swelled with a newfound compassion as I saw the destitute congregation emerging from the nearby bridges and alleyways. Several dozen people of all ages and shades made their way to the makeshift buffet line set up by a local street ministry. Most of those on this ministry team had survived hard times themselves, so relating to the homeless attendees was easy for them.

During worship, which was blasted from a very retro boom box with a CD player and a karaoke microphone, I sensed the Lord tap me on the shoulder. He drew my attention to a particular young woman.

"I want you to minister to her," I sensed him say.

I got so excited! She was about twenty-five years old with matted blonde hair, torn and dirty clothing, and no shoes. Her Christmas-themed fleece pajama bottoms were at least two sizes too big, and the shadows under her eyes gave away her recent bender.

My heart hurt with the compassion of the Lord as I saw her brokenness. It was hard for me not to weep as I asked if I could pray with her. She eagerly accepted my invitation, and we sat down together on a parking lot curb away from the crowd.

As I took her hands, I saw the movie screen of my mind come to life with scenes of her past. The Lord supernaturally downloaded information about her that I could not have possibly known, and I told her what I saw. Then all of my prayer training kicked in, and I led her through lots of forgiveness, repentance, and renunciation of the lies she was believing. Both of us were wrecked as we wept and rejoiced and marveled. And when we were done, she had seen and heard Jesus for herself, and he had shown her a picture of a freshly cleaned slate.

I knew in that moment that this was what I was put on this earth to do.

I had discovered my destiny.

Lord, I rejoice at how you have led me to destiny. I forgive and release my mom for how she judged my stepping into ministry as a big mistake, and I forgive her for having no grid for your provision. I praise and thank you, Lord, for allowing me to minister your heart to your children. In your holy name I pray, amen.

Chapter Thirty-Three
GRIEF

The liquid leaking out of the corners of my eyes couldn't have surprised me any more than a stranger dumping water on my head.

"What in the world is this?!" I whispered to myself.

I had been standing in line at the local southern-style cafeteria where I had seen a lady whose high forehead and wide smile bore a striking resemblance to my mom. She shuffled with a walker like Mom's, but that didn't prevent her from gushing several lavish compliments over the small army of children one mother was corralling. I had seen Mom share these kinds of accolades to strangers many times.

Then a younger woman, presumably the shuffler's daughter, gently took her mother's elbow and escorted her safely to a seat. I had done that with Mom often in recent years.

Only this time, I didn't have a living mother anymore. It had been several months since her passing. Those months had been tactical and busy, helping Dad sort and donate her clothing, sort and sell her tubs of craft supplies and décor, and sort and distribute sixty years' worth of classical and religious piano music. It all felt cathartic, satisfying, and necessary. It felt nothing like grief.

I had easily shed tears at her memorial service, but those were more out of compassion for the pain I felt around me than for myself. I had shed tears a few weeks after that service as I recounted to a close friend the tragedy that was my mom's final few dying days. But those tears were out of anger at the injustice she experienced at the hands of big medicine.

This grief thing that came like a rogue wave was different.

It's hard to learn to grieve someone you once hated. But I am learning. It's true that I had discovered how, through the Lord's supernatural healing, to release the hatred and to love and enjoy my mom for the final seven years of her life. But before that, I'd had close to forty years of hatred for her. I had also been raised in a family that regarded any expression of grief as a sign of weakness. Not once was I ever shown what healthy grief looked like. Weeping at a funeral was considered hysterical behavior in my world.

I have also begun to learn that part of the grieving process must include grieving what wasn't and what won't be. These come to mind every time I hear a woman gush about her mother, "My mom is my best friend in the whole world!"

My mom wasn't anyone's best friend, not in a healthy and mutually beneficial sort of way.

Or, "The one person I know I can always trust for wise advice is my mom. I had the most amazing mother. I can only hope to be a mom like her."

These were simply not my narrative. So each time I hear words like these, grief forces me to acknowledge its existence yet again.

Thankfully I have learned not to wallow there. I know how to take these emotions to the Lord, to acknowledge the negative feelings that come with unpleasant reminders, and to exchange them for peace, comfort, and gratitude. If I don't choose this every single time, I won't heal.

It makes sense now why my eyes began leaking at the buffet checkout. For the very first time in my entire life, I actually missed my mom. Although it took a while to comprehend, I now know this is perfectly normal.

In my fifty-plus years of living before Mom passed, I have had countless shopping trips, dining experiences, and doctor's visits. I cannot think of a single time in all of those experiences where I noticed a woman helping her elderly mother, guiding her softly by the elbow, easing her mother backward into a car, or wiping her mother's messy chin.

I notice it everywhere now, and I allow myself to miss my mom. And I gladly let the tears come.

Jesus, I choose to forgive my mom, my dad, and all of my grandparents for treating expressions of grief as weakness. I forgive them for never teaching me healthy grief, and I forgive them for the effects this has had on my life. I choose to forgive Mom for all that wasn't and couldn't be. Lord, I give you permission to continue to show me how to grieve in a healthy way, as I give myself permission to grieve. Amen.

Chapter Thirty-Four
SANDRA'S DAUGHTER

"You must be Sandra's daughter."

The way the hunched, elderly lady spoke, one would have thought I was the daughter of Mother Teresa herself. I was in my mid-twenties, singing at a church. I felt like hissing at this stranger's connection of me to my mother, but I plastered a smile.

"That's right! Sandra's my mom!"

I hoped my boastful tone sounded believable. The old woman gushed on about Mom for hours. Or minutes. Either way, torture for me. Every time this happened, my inner self screamed.

You have no idea who you're really talking about! If you knew the truth, you would hate her too!

My twenties were spent mostly in fierce independence and flippant rebellion. Having married my high school boyfriend merely two days after my eighteenth birthday (because Mom couldn't stop me), I was having babies, climbing a corporate ladder, and definitely not needing nor missing my mother.

She had tried to do the grandma thing right after my first was born, flying six hundred miles to "help," But since I wasn't complying with her demand to be the center of attention, she threw a pity party, packed up in a huff and left early. Her dramatic departure left me alone with a colicky, angry newborn and an absent husband. It also left me sad and bitter.

Mom and I may have talked on the phone once or twice a month in those years, but I don't believe she noticed, since her favored son still lived with her. Catering to his every want was fulfilling enough for her.

Ministers, therapists, and even Jesus himself all counsel us never to make inner vows, because our enemy satan holds us to every word. We don't know this in the moment of course. But there is a sense of power, albeit false, in regularly declaring that "I will NEVER be like her."

But DNA, family patterns, and behavioral norms all have a way of converging to make a mockery of such a vow. Then the shock comes at my passing thirty-year-old reflection in the mirror seeing Mom staring back at me in the glass. This just made me angrier. So the more I hated her, the more I hated myself.

But the motive for this question is not the same when

it's heard in a hospital.

"Are you Sandra's daughter?" asked the serious man in the long white coat.

The question came from an ICU doctor who had been trying to keep Mom's COPD-laden lungs from collapsing. I answered in the affirmative.

He nodded gently. "We're doing everything we can, so we just need to wait and see if her body responds. Double pneumonia with COPD really makes a mess in there. You can stay with her as long as you want to. Just let us know if you need anything."

I'm so very grateful that the Lord did not allow me in my anger to choose rejection over compassionate concern when she became really sick this first time. She had contracted pneumonia after ignoring her symptoms for too long, and her lungs were rebelling against her. Watching her fight to inhale against the infection trying to drown her was horrifying and traumatic. In one particular moment where she was struggling to breathe, I believed I was watching her die in front of me. It hurt my heart to see how terrified she was. After that, she ended up in a medically induced coma hooked up to a ventilator for almost two weeks.

She was only given fifty-fifty odds of surviving that illness. She came through it; praise be to God. But when she learned that she had lost almost two weeks of her life, she was shocked and retraumatized. She felt so guilty for taking up so much of everyone's time trying to keep her alive, she believed she owed God and everyone else. It broke my heart to see her partner with shame after all of that.

Perhaps the timing of this brush with death was another little piece of the complex puzzle coming together for the healing of my heart. Many people sober up quickly in the face of death as the reality of what was almost lost sets in. I am so grateful now that we were granted more time with her.

As I tell my story today wherever anyone will listen, I emphasize the sacredness and gravity of fleeting time. Coming to peace and releasing the past after someone has already died just isn't the same as choosing to deal with it while they are still present. Regret is an evil gift that keeps on giving.

It didn't occur to me until now that I will probably never hear the question about being Sandra's daughter again.

The last time I heard it was on Mother's Day, a few months after she passed into eternity. The prior year, before her death, I had been planning to surprise Mom on Mother's Day by singing a song called "Alabaster Box" at the church she attended. It was one of her favorite late '90s inspirational Christian songs, which she would have loved to hear. But she was gone before Mother's Day came. So in her honor, I decided to sing it for her church congregation.

As I rehearsed in her little historic church sanctuary

before the service, a few devout early birds trickled into the rickety wooden pews. After my practice run was finished, a frail woman with curly, cotton-white hair and twinkling eyes approached me.

She took my hands in hers, and fighting back a flood of tears, she leaned close to me.

"You must be Sandra's daughter. Oh, we just loved her so much."

In truth, with honor and gratitude, grief and joy, I hugged her.

"Yes ma'am," I answered. "I'm sure you did."

And I did too.

As I left that little church and stepped into the bright spring sunshine, my mind drifted back to that last, beautiful sunset with Mom. I felt myself smile with deep gratitude.

Yes, I am Sandra's daughter.

Lord, I repent for every time I dishonored and hated my mom with my thoughts and my words, and I forgive myself. I repent for the inner vows that I made, and I renounce those vows. I choose to forgive my mom for giving outsiders a better version of herself than she gave to us. I nail all of the hatred and resentment to the cross, and Lord, I ask you to cleanse and heal the wounds in my soul. Amen.

THE EMPTY CHAIR EXERCISE

*I*f reading about this journey has opened up the possibility of your starting your own similar journey, you can begin right now.

One of the most powerful and effective ways to process childhood wounds and lies is to spend time identifying specifics such as harmful words, actions, or omissions, and the emotions connected to those. These specifics become the list of things we choose to forgive and release to the Lord. We cannot heal what we do not reveal.

Spend some dedicated time to complete the details of each suggested topic below. This bulleted list is presented as specific to your mother and father, but these topics can apply to anyone in your life with whom the relationship is unhealthy or to those who caused you harm. This could include siblings, spouses, in-laws, managers, and even our grown children. Freedom from wounded relationships is not limited to immediate family. Grace extends to all.

It's also important to recognize that sometimes, the person we haven't yet forgiven is already deceased. For the purposes of this kind of emotional healing, the fact that they have died has no bearing on my need to forgive them. Unforgiveness is unforgiveness, whether or not the offender has passed away. We forgive to release ourselves, and we will always be bound in an ungodly way to those we will not forgive, whether or not they are living.

You will likely experience emotion during this exercise. Don't let that deter you from pursuing your freedom. Humans were wired by God to experience the full range of emotions, and we must not allow a fear of emotion to prevent us from healthy processing. If necessary, a skilled Christian therapist can help the process of allowing blocked emotions to flow in a healthy way. If you fear becoming overwhelmed with emotion, ask a trusted, healthy Christian friend to come alongside you in support.

Because this kind of emotional healing is a journey, allow yourself to focus on one person at a time. You may be tempted to construct multiple lists for multiple offenders and address them all together as a group. This may seem efficient, but it will not be effective. Unless the people you need to forgive are a handful of former friends who were all involved in a single embarrassing but relatively minor incident, take your time, one person at a time.

It is critical to understand that forgiveness and reconciliation are often mutually exclusive. Forgiveness may not always result in restored relationship (and may be dangerous in some situations). It takes two healthy, humble, mutually respectful people to maintain a relationship. One can fully forgive and release a toxic, violent abuser without removing healthy boundaries. We forgive for ourselves, not for the other person. We cannot forgive in expectation of justice, payback, or retribution. Those belong solely to the Lord. We also cannot forgive expecting the offender to change as a result. We can only change ourselves.

Using pen and paper, typing into a computer, or whatever method allows you to record a lot of detail, build your highly specific list of everything connected to the parental figures who raised you. Ask the Lord to bring things to mind that you buried or chose to forget. Be certain to include the emotions you felt in connection to what was said or done, whether or not your rational mind believes that your emotions were appropriate. Use the below bullet points as a starting point. Leave nothing out.

- Their negative patterns or self-destructive choices
- Their specific actions that wounded me or others

- Words or phrases they used that wounded me or others
- Emotional or material things I needed that they didn't give
- Anything else about them that comes to mind
- Specific negative emotions I feel toward them as a result of these things

In addition to everything your offender has done, it's critical to acknowledge your own failures and poor choices in anything that happened. So on a separate list, allow yourself to name your sins and failures as well. If you harbored bitterness or rebellion, write those down. If you know that you are guilty of cheating, lying, abandonment, or abuse, name those things. Brutal honesty with yourself is critical here. If you should've apologized and didn't, or you spent years in vengeance or hatred, list those things. The Bible specifies that if we are faithful to confess, he is faithful to forgive and cleanse. This kind of healing process would be incomplete without repentance.

When your lists are fully complete, find a quiet place free from interruption. Spend a few moments preparing your heart and connecting with the Lord in whatever way is comfortable for you. Listening to worshipful music, reading your Bible, or meditating on gratitude can all be helpful.

Using your mind's eye, imagine that the person you need to forgive is sitting in a chair right in front of you.

Precisely how you envision them (older, younger, etc.) is not terribly relevant unless they happened to be especially harmful to you around a specific age. As best as you can, imagine the offender in the state or age when they were most harmful to you. Once you see the person in your mind's eye, taking hold of your written list, begin to forgive each and every detail on your list, including the emotions you have identified.

It might sound something like, "Mom, I choose to forgive you, for every affair you had. You dishonored your marriage vows, and you destroyed my dad by your cheating. He didn't deserve that. Mom, I forgive you, for putting Dad down all the time, for embarrassing him, and for laughing at him in front of his family. I forgive you for the hurt this caused me. Mom, I forgive you, for forcing me to lie to Dad about all of your boyfriends. That wasn't fair to me, and I forgive you for how gross that made me feel."

As you are moving through your list, check off or strike through what you've written as you forgive it. This process will ensure that nothing is left out. If new things come to mind in the midst of the exercise, by all means, include them and include the connected emotions.

Your next step is to move to the list of your own offenses and failures that you identified. We must repent (agree with God's perspective) for our wrongs, and forgive ourselves, if we want to be free of them. So in your mind's eye, with your offender still sitting in the empty chair in front of you, imagine Jesus himself standing right next to them. With the Lord as your focus, confess everything to him.

This might sound something like, "Lord, I repent for how I constantly butted heads with Mom, and I repent for every time I cussed her out and made her cry. Jesus, I repent for stealing from her and blaming my sister, and I forgive myself for doing that. I repent for making Mom feel responsible when I flunked out of school. Lord, I repent and I ask you to forgive me for being rude when she broke her leg and I had to drive her around. I forgive myself for being so mean to her." As you address everything, check every item off until nothing is left.

When your lists have been completely forgiven or confessed, and every item is checked off, use your mind's eye to see yourself releasing the offender to the Lord. Imagine Jesus coming to the chair where the offender has been seated, and see him lead the offender away to deal with them however he sees fit. Imagine yourself and the offender standing at the foot of the cross, and see yourself leaving the offender there and walking away. Ask the Lord to bring an image to your mind of what it looks like for you to fully release this person to him, and let the Lord play that out. The goal of releasing them to the Lord is to accept that they are his full responsibility, not yours.

Once you have forgiven and confessed and released, take the lists you used in this process and destroy them. If they were on paper, tear them up or burn them. If they were on a computer or other device, delete the file, then find any recycling or trash folder and permanently delete it. As you destroy these lists of wrongs, use your mind's eye to imagine Jesus taking every connected negative emotion away from you. The Lord may give you a mental picture of reaching his hand into your heart and removing the pain. You may envision the negative emotions floating out of your heart into the hands of Jesus. Ask the Lord to show the eyes of your heart what it looks like for him to take those from you. This step can be a powerful, radically healing time with the Lord.

Finally, we want to make an exchange with the Lord. For every negative, painful emotion that was just released to him, we ask him to fill us with something from him in exchange. We can ask him questions such as, "Lord, what does all of this mean for me?" Or "Lord, now that I have given all of that to you, what would you like to give me in exchange?" Or "Lord, what do I need from you right now?" Those negative emotions have taken up valuable space, and that space must be filled with what the Lord has for us. When we ask him, he will never leave us unfilled.

Thank you for joining me on this healing journey!

From the depths of my heart, thank you for taking the time to become a part of this transformative journey toward healing and freedom. It is my sincere hope that the words within this book have touched your spirit and sparked a desire for own lasting change.

Reviews are critical to the sharing of this message to others, so I thank you in advance for taking a moment to write a review on Amazon, Goodreads, or other platforms where this book is available.

As a token of my gratitude, I invite you to download a powerful resource that has personally impacted me on my path to healing: the "Daily Spiritual Warfare Prayer". Adapted from an original prayer by Victor Matthews, this scripturally-based prayer has been an effective daily source of strength, identity, and authority in my life for many years.

Follow the link below to download your complimentary "Daily Spiritual Warfare Prayer" and embark on your own journey toward identity and authority in Christ.

Download now from:

https://www.lambornauthor.ink/freecontent

RESOURCES

If you would like additional resources to help you to start your own journey from hatred to love, from pain to peace, or from trauma to healing, please connect with one of these incredible ministries. I bless your journey. —Nanci Lamborn

Beth Shalom Inner Healing Ministries
https://bethshalomtexas.com/

Bethel Sozo Ministry
https://www.bethelsozo.com/

Christian Healing Ministries
https://www.christianhealingmin.org/

College of Athens Prayer Ministry
https://collegeofathens.edu/what-is-prayer-ministry/

Freedom in Christ Ministries
https://www.ficm.org

Immanuel Prayer Network
https://www.immanuelapproach.com

Orbis Ministries Prayer Network
https://orbisprayer.org/

ADDITIONAL RECOMMENDED READING

The Bait of Satan – John Bevere

Deep Wounds, Deep Healing – Charles Kraft

Forgiving Forward – Bruce and Toni Hebel

Victory Over the Darkness – Neil T. Anderson

END NOTES

25. INIQUITY

1. Selwyn R. Stevens, PhD, "Prayer of Release for Freemasons & Their Descendants" (PDF), Jubilee Resources, Jubilee Resources International, 2017.

31. HOLY ANGUISH

1. John Ramirez, *Armed and Dangerous* (Missouri, US: Chosen Books, 2017).

ABOUT THE AUTHOR

Nanci Lamborn, born and raised in the buckle of the Bible belt, spent twenty-five years in corporate America. After experiencing firsthand the supernatural transformation of forgiveness and inner healing prayer, Nanci's journey took a significant turn as she embraced her calling into Christian ministry. As an ordained minister and licensed chaplain, she devotes her full-time efforts to helping individuals break free from their past, drawing from her own profoundly healing experiences.

Nanci is also a devoted wife, mother, and an immensely proud grandmother. She finds joy in camping, savoring coffee, cultivating her garden, and tending to her backyard chickens. Her passion is to see others walking free into their destiny, knowing and loving who God created them to be.

Made in the USA
Columbia, SC
02 April 2024